"At last! A book about therapy a lay person can understand. *From Worry to Wellness* explains beautifully and simply how therapy works and gives us the good news that there is hope and help out there. If you have ever felt anxious or anxiety, read this book at once."

Fannie Flagg
Actress, author of *Fried Green Tomatoes at the Whistle Stop Cafe*

"Authentic stories, the commentary by the authors, and action plans all make *From Worry to Wellness* a valuable resource. For persons already committed to growth and human development, it enriches and reaffirms their endeavors. For persons who have yet to address their pain, it offers encouragement and incentive to begin. For the general reader, it provides a sound, reliable approach to constructive therapy. I strongly encourage college students, especially those preparing for careers in human services, to read this worthwhile book."

Teresa M. Houlihan, Ph.D.
Providence College

From Worry to Wellness

How 21 People Changed Their Lives

Ruth Morrison &
Dawn Radtke

XXIII
TWENTY-THIRD PUBLICATIONS
Mystic, Connecticut

Twenty-Third Publications
185 Willow Street
P.O. Box 180
Mystic, CT 06355
(203) 536-2611

ISBN 0-89622-443-0
Library of Congress Catalog Card Number 90-70559

Acknowledgments

We want to express our thanks to the people who wrote their stories for this book. The names they chose for themselves are listed in the next pages. Their willingness to write about their pain and suffering as well as their journey to wholeness is a gift to us all.

We also want to thank the people listed below who were kind enough to read our manuscript and offer suggestions whereby this book could be more helpful to you.

Lee Lester
Sue Simmons M.A.
Mooie Slater M.S.W.
Dorothy Vergeer M.A.

Contents

PART TWO—HOW THERAPY WORKS

PART THREE—CHANGING YOUR LIFE

From Worry to Wellness

How 21 People Changed Their Lives

Introduction

As we look around us, we see many people worrying about life rather than living, people who believe the meaning of life is to be found in "getting ahead," "getting what I want," going for the thrills and kicks in life. If these are the goals, there's certainly plenty of excitement in our world, plenty of opportunities for self-aggrandisement, and many say that the pursuit of happiness is what it's all about. Excitement, pursuit of happiness, and self-aggrandisement; but are they truly life-giving? Will they fill us with a sense of vitality, hope, and joy? We think not, and we believe that those who worry about finding them are looking for hope in all the wrong places. Where are the people of joy? Joy is that special gift to those who are at peace with themselves, compassionate with others, and thankful for all that life has given them. Instead of men and women living joyful lives, we see people worrying about making sense in a seemingly senseless world.

Is there another way to live? Can we really choose to stop worrying and opt for wellness? How can we even talk about wellness in a world that seems to be destroying itself in death?

How can we keep from worrying? The well-known Viennese psychiatrist, Dr. Victor Frankl, asked that same question while he was in a Nazi concentration camp. Frankl found hope and reason for living in the midst of that hell. He came to what he later called "Self-transcendence." In 1948, Frankl published a book about his life in "the camp." *Man's Search for Meaning* became a best seller as thousands of people searched for meaning in the hopelessness and insanity of World War II. Recently, Frankl's book has been rediscovered, perhaps because many of us believe our time is a time of hopelessness and insanity. Unlike leaders of business, commerce, and politics, Frankl invites us to take hope not in systems, but in Self-transcendence, by which he means finding meaning within ourselves in whatever circumstances we live. Frankl does not deny the destructive power of international conflict, crime, oppression, drugs, starvation, and disease. He says, however, that in the midst of the most agonizing and devastating life, people—you and I—can live with hope and meaning.

How can you find this hope, this meaning, this Self-transcendence? This is what our book is about.

For over twenty years the authors have counseled hundreds of people who have lived with meaninglessness, agony, devastation, and despair. They came to us (professional therapists) with the hope that they could change their lives. They did!

Those who came to us presented a variety of problems. They represented a wide range of ages, economic, social, and educational backgrounds. Some had been hospitalized in institutions for the mentally ill and a number had been heavily medicated by their psychiatrists or other physicians. Some came with relatively simple problems. Some were in therapy for long periods of time, others for only a few sessions. Among them, we chose a few and asked them to tell you their stories in their own words. Then we added our comments to what they had written. Next, we drew some conclusions about what they did while they were in treatment, and how they made choices to change from despair to hope and joy. This book, then, begins with their stories told in their own words and our comments as their therapists who worked alongside each of them while they changed their lives.[1]

In Part Two, we describe how we work as therapists, the development of children (since so many problems people have as adults come from their childhood experiences), and "Little Work or Re-parenting," our work with people who need healing from childhood pain, suffering, and deprivation.

---

[1] Most of these stories are written by women. It is regrettable that our culture teaches us that "big boys don't cry." Men who suffer emotional pain usually believe they must bear that pain silently and not seek therapuetic help.

In Part Three, "Changing Your Life," you will find a number of very specific suggestions for making your changes. These suggestions have been used successfully by many people with whom we have worked and we hope they will be useful to you. As you think about the changes you want to make in your life, we believe that it will be important for you to understand your feelings, especially those that are painful or cause you to worry. We have written a long section to show you how to do this and how to deal with uncomfortable feelings so that you can have the joy and wellness you deserve.

We have written this book for you. The choices you make today determines the quality of your life tomorrow. Remember, "Today is the first day of the rest of your life."

PART ONE

CHANGED LIVES

Midlife Crisis

ALICE

My first acquaintance with Alice was in one of my workshops for women who wanted to discover more about themselves and their relationships. After the workshop finished, Alice came to a short-term therapy group and finally chose to be part of an ongoing group. Alice's problems focused around her anger and poor self-image. In group therapy she could gain support and acceptance for the changes she wanted to make both in self-image and relationships.

Alice had a pleasant personality, smiled a lot, took care of other people, and was very much overweight. My guess was that her smiles and caretaking covered her sadness, and her obesity was a way of slowly killing herself without actually committing suicide. She was in touch with her anger and felt guilty about being so full of rage, but she was not aware of her fears, the depth of her sadness, or her unconscious determination to kill herself.

Alice's Story

When I think of my life before therapy, I think of a lot of pain, anguish, anger, and lack of understanding why my life was so miserable. I had an excellent education and a loving family, and come from a loving family. I had a husband, four children, and a job, but I was totally miserable. I could not understand why. I would wring my hands. I would pace. I would pray. I worked at a church, and I can remember going into the sanctuary, falling on my knees and crying, "God! What is the matter? I know there's more. I know there's something missing in my life, but I don't know what it is. I am so miserable!" I found myself lashing out or being very passive and depressed. If I saw two people standing talking together at the church, I knew they were talking about me and my inability to do my job. A perfectionist, I was working forty hours a week in a twenty-hour job. Nevertheless I knew that they were talking about how I was not doing everything I should be doing. It never dawned on me that they surely had more important things to talk about than me and my performance.

I needed constant assurance that I was doing an okay job, but I couldn't get enough of it. Or, if I got it, I would say, "If only." I remember when I was teaching school I received a note enclosed in my contract. The note was a personal, handwritten one from the superintendent saying, "Many, many thanks for the marvelous job you're doing in our music department." And my reaction was, "If he knew that I started only fourteen violins at Central Junior High this year, he'd never say that."

I wouldn't let my cup be filled. My self-worth was all based on performance because I felt I had absolutely no value as a human being. I was the middle child of three. I had a very, very smart, talented, older brother and a very cute younger sister and that's what I heard about when I heard people talk about our family— the older brother, the younger sister. I never heard anything good about myself. When I say "never," that's because I blocked out the positive things they said. I'm sure my family had good things to say about me, but I didn't hear them. I only heard what was good about Mary and Fred. What was good about Alice passed right by me. I saw myself as ugly. I saw myself as someone that nobody would want to spend time with. I saw myself as someone that people just tolerated. I discounted totally the people who did care about me, thinking that they only cared about me because they were nice people, not because of who I was. I was also sure that I was the only person who felt this way. I was sure that everyone else was self-confident, able to do things better than I could do them. I was second-rate and they were first-rate.

I felt as if I were in a cage, pacing back and forth, growling, snapping, and then going to lie in the corner to nap and be passive. Then I would get up and again, growl, snarl, and lash out. But there was always someone to crack a whip over me and put me back where I belonged. There was always somebody to say what needed to be said to put me back in my place—back in my cage.

For years I had done nothing to solve my problems because I saw them as something I had to live with. That was just who I was. That's how I fit in the world, and there was nothing that could be done about it. I just endured and prayed for a miracle.

That's what I actually got. A lady at the church, whom I wouldn't even call a friend at the time, came up to me and said, "One of the local colleges is having a program to help women step out into the world. How about going with me and seeing what it's all about?" So, I took five dollars out of the grocery money and went with her. That day was the beginning of a new life for me. That was when I first began to believe I could change, I could be different. It had never dawned on me before that I had any choice or had any say in decisions that affected me. I felt the decisions had all been made by someone bigger than I and that there was nothing I could do about them. This was the way life was going to be, and that was all there was to it.

The program was a three-week workshop, and at the end of three weeks, the leader invited anyone who wanted to to become part of a therapy group. I decided it was important for me to be part of that group, so each week I would take five dollars out of the grocery money and go to therapy.

I began to talk about my anger. The therapist wanted me to act out that anger, and asked me what it was I wanted to do. I said, "What I want to do is pick up that chair and break it." She said, "Go ahead." (Several pieces of old furniture had been provided for us to break up if we wanted to.) I picked up the chair, hit it on the floor and broke it into three pieces. That was the beginning of release for me, release of the anger that I had allowed to keep me captive for over forty years. It was the first rattle on my cage that was eventually going to free me from captivity.

The most important thing that I began to learn was that *I* had made all the decisions that put me where I was, and having made those decisions myself, I could redecide them. I did not have control over everything that happened in my life, but I did have control over how I handled those happenings. Until that time, it was as if everything was written in stone. It could not be changed. When I realized I could change old decisions, I was ready to go forth full-tilt. Some decisions were harder to change than others. It was hard for me to realize that I might be lovable—very difficult. Where I came from, if you weren't the smartest you weren't smart at all. If you weren't the prettiest you weren't pretty at all. And now I had a chance to remake those decisions, change my own reality, change my way of thinking about myself and how I fit in the world. This was the most important and valuable lesson that I learned in therapy.

The major stages in my therapy were all geared toward getting me out of my cage. In the beginning, it was learning self-esteem, building my own self-esteem, becoming aware of the Child in me that was so hurt, the Parent in me that was so hurtful, and becoming aware that I wasn't even using my Adult function when I was thinking about myself. Putting those together was the first step in realizing there was a way out.

The next thing I had to do was to work on my anger. I was so enraged! Week after week, I would pound pillows, scream, holler. It felt as if there was a big well inside of me with no bottom. It was absolutely filled with anger and the anger went into infinity. Being able to express this rage, and becoming aware of what I was angry about (recalling some of the things that happened when I was young), began to ease my pain. I remembered the battles I used to have with my father. I was told that the parent's job is to form a child, and the stronger willed that child is, the harder the parent has to work to form that child in the way the parent thinks he or she should be formed. This is the kind of child I was, I think.

My father had a difficult time making me into the child he wanted me to be. In fact, he never did. He was never physically abusive, but I used to get spanked very often as a child. But with all my spankings he was not able to do what my mother was able to do with a few words. My gentle, loving, tolerant mother who, when I was nine years old, finally in desperation said to me, "If you don't stop acting that way, no one is ever going to like you." I was terrified. I fought going in that cage for my father, but when my mother said those words, I gave in. I entered the cage by becoming what she wanted me to be. I went into the cage angry, hurt, scared.

In therapy, I recognized where my anger came from, and then I knew that there was a bottom to that well of anger and I *could* get myself out of my cage. After I dealt with my old anger and had a pretty good handle on it, I realized that my anger had covered over my fear. I had been so busy being angry that I never realized how frightened I was.

When I wanted to work on my fear, I began a very special piece of work in therapy, one that I remember as perhaps the single most important work that I did. My therapist said, "Is it time to come out of your cage?" I said, "Yeah, I think so, but I don't know how." She said, "Okay, close your eyes. If you're ready to come out, if you think it's safe and you want to come out, tell us about your cage—describe it." I closed my eyes and told the group the cage was square. About as big as a living room and had a door on it. I never went near the door, but I would go to the sides of the cage and shake and rattle it, but I couldn't get out. The therapist had me visualize doing this, rattling the cage, doing everything I could lashing out, and then she said, "Where's the door?" I told her the door was at the end. She said, "Go to the door." and I did. She said, "Try it." I tried it and it opened. I opened the door. The therapist said, "Are you ready to come out?" And I said, "I think so, but I want to know that if I step out I can come back." She said, "The door is yours to open or to close. You can come back if you want to." So I came out of the cage and in my visualization, coming out of the cage with my eyes closed, there was immediate sunlight, green grass, flowers, trees, and singing birds. The sun was shining beautifully and the air was so clear. I could breathe and I felt free. I walked around for a long time telling everyone what I saw and felt. Then I said, "I want to go back into my cage." I went back, but I left the door open so that I could go in and out anytime I wanted to. I rarely put myself back in the cage, but when I did, I always knew I could open the door any time I chose. I did a lot of forgiving after that. I had blamed my parents for putting me in the cage, and now I knew that I had put myself there.

From that time on, there were a lot of "Wows" in my therapy and a good deal of awe when I found other issues that had not been in my earlier awareness. I made many decisions to free myself even more. I always knew that I was safe. I always knew that my therapist wouldn't take me any place I wasn't ready to go, and I always knew that she would go with me if I needed help. I felt comfortable and very thankful.

In the years since therapy I have changed my life in many positive ways. I relate differently to my parents. I have changed my relationship with my children. I became a parent in a loving, caring way instead of being a tyrant who demanded my children to do what I wanted them to do because I knew best. I have become much more relaxed within myself. I have become more tolerant with myself and other people. I find that I can understand other people's views, not always agreeing, but understanding and accepting. I am not as critical of others as I used to be. I can live in the world as a grown person, an adult. I belong in the world.

I now lead workshops in "Family Communication" and also workshops in "Building Self-Esteem." I talk to fairly large groups and I know that I am listened to and respected. I am able to listen instead of giving all the information. I am a good workshop leader. I now work for senior services, and I find that I relate well to senior citizens because I listen to them. I hear their pain. I hear their joy. I know that these pains and joys are theirs, not mine.

My life has become a joyful place to be. I have problems. I solve them with the tools I learned in therapy. I have troubles. I feel my pain. I accept it. And I go on. When I feel depressed, I know that there is another side to the depression. Whatever it is, even though I may not know the cause, I am not going to be mired in it forever. My life has become whole. I fit. I belong. And I do believe that God answered my prayer when I said, "God! Help me, help me." I believe that he sent Nancy to me to say, "Alice, let's go to this workshop." He sent me to my therapist.

Today as I'm thinking back to that other time before therapy, it seems as if it wasn't really me. It was somebody else. It was almost a different life, a different time, a different space. Strange. My kids used to talk about "Mom before, Mom after," i.e., when I first started in therapy and they'd see the changes, and now I think about "before" and "after." I know that everything I ever did, every decision I made, and every re-decision I made led me to where I am right now. I don't regret where I was, because I know that was where I needed to be at one time. I'm just grateful to everybody who has been in it with me. But, I'm most grateful that I'm on the other side now.

After Alice had faced her fear, come out of her cage, built her self-esteem, and made a decision to live her own life instead of being controlled by other people, we dealt with her obesity. I finally asked her what would happen if she kept putting on weight. In a fantasy exercise, she said, "I'll just blow up in lots of little pieces and then I'll be no more." It was at this point that the group and the therapist assured her that she was loved for herself and not for her performance. Alice took a moment to absorb what we had said. She looked around, and then made her decision to stop killing herself with food and obesity and start using food for health, wholeness, and life. Neither Alice nor the therapist had a goal of ideal weight. What she weighed would be determined by health and life, not by destruction and death. Today, Alice is comfortable with her weight and her appearance and especially with her decision to live.

BARBARA

Barbara tried hard to be strong and not accept her real feelings. As a result she felt anxious or depressed most of the time. The first time I saw her, she said she was confused and tense. She thought she was in a hopeless situation and helpless to do anything about it. Obviously bright and attractive, and with a delightful sense of humor, Barbara was stuck. She had recently divorced, had teenage boys living at home, and was ambivalent about her job. She was aware of being frustrated, but not aware of the depth of anger or sadness.

Barbara's Story

(Part One)

I had had a terrrible marriage and had been taking Valium for ten years as well as Elavil for a shorter time, when I started group therapy with another therapist. After I left my husband, and proceeded with getting a divorce, I stopped taking medication. I had very few side effects when I stopped taking the medication, and I left that group. When I first came to see one of the authors about joining one of her groups, I felt unable to cope by myself. I was depressed and anxious.

My therapy with her was more structured than the other group I had been in. This helped each of us take responsibility for getting something out of the group. It also enabled all group members to get attention and time to get their needs met.

She listened to each person very carefully and seemed to respect what we said. Many therapists seem to see pathology in normal behavior simply because it is in keeping with their diagnosis. She did not do this.

I learned from listening to others in the group. I learned that I was not the only person with my kind of problems. I also learned to cope with a great variety of problems. This was accomplished by watching other people work. Sometimes other people brought up things that I probably would never have thought of discussing myself, even though I had similar concerns.

The most valuable thing I learned was that I can take care of myself. I gained a broad perspective on life that I feel sure I would never have had otherwise.

At first I was afraid to say anything, though I listened and learned. Next, I remember having some very strong emotional experiences that probably resulted in more growth than in any time in my therapy. I realized that some experiences in my childhood were not as they had seemed at the time. I felt real support from the others in the group. My re-parenting experiences were a part of this stage.

I especially remember one time when our therapist was reading several of us a story from a children's book. We were all sitting, either on her lap or at her feet. At one point she responded to something I said by saying, "You have very good ideas." It had never occured to me before that I could have good ideas. *That one chance remark, simply a product of good parenting, has been a wonder in my life ever since. I really can have good ideas.*

Then came a final phase in which I probably learned more from others in the group than I did from the work I did myself. I was fascinated by the process. This was also a time of *reinforcement* of what I had learned for myself, as well as *support* from the group for my new ways of coping. At this point our therapist decided to move out of town. Although she gave us four months notice, this was very hard for me. I was not ready to let go.

However, I was no longer depressed. I was better able to cope and to live independently, I had a much broader view of life and I performed better on the job and was a better mother to my children. I was decidedly happier.

Barbara's Story
(Part Two)

About five years after my therapist left town, I found myself in a very different situation indeed, and I sought her help a second time.

I had fallen and hurt my head, and had several other physical problems which either brought on or contributed to manic depression. Having a severe mental condition of this sort was new to me. It was shocking, and a terrible blow to my self-esteem. In addition, I could not seem to find competent medical help. I was put on Lithium and my memory was badly affected. (Recent findings have shown that memory loss can be a side effect of Lithium.) No one seemed to be concerned about the fact that this loss of memory would ruin my career. I sought more effective help, but with such a defective memory it was difficult to handle any of my affairs very well. After taking a year off, I called my old therapist again and arranged to come where she lived for a short time so that I could have more therapy with her.

The therapy I had received when manic depression was first diagnosed was done by a very experienced and highly regarded psychologist in my home town. She had been a professor of psychology and was also very successful in private practice and in a clinic that she owned and hired other psychologists to work in. But she treated me as though I was not able to think, to make my own decisions, know what I was feeling, or know how I experienced what was wrong with me. I realize now that this is the way we frequently treat people who are or who have been seriously mentally ill. *We are treated like children; however, we are not loved like children.*

I became angry with her because she was unwilling to believe me when I said my memory was poor. It was my external situation that was problematic to me, but she kept seeing it as an internal problem. Indeed, I am not perfect, and I have quirks that need ironing out, but the problems resulting from my external world were the most pressing for me at that time.

Therapy with my old therapist was quite different. She listened to me and acted on what I said with the assumption I was telling the truth. She helped me to talk to myself in ways to relieve my anxiety, not to increase it. She had me experiment with different ways to improve my memory. Some of these were practical things to help me function better, for example, writing things down. Some were a means of getting to possible causes, for example, not having caffeine and watching my sugar intake. She also helped me check out additional medical resources, for example, New Medico, a national organization which specializes only in the effects and treatment of head injuries, and the Lithium Clinic in Madison, Wisconsin for the most recent information about the side effects of Lithium. She stayed with me emotionally and saw me through some bad times. She went at my pace, with my problems as I experienced them.

The most valuable thing I learned this time was to trust myself—to listen to myself, just as she had listened to me. She helped me to break out of the mold—the mold I am so inclined to fall into that I allow other people to create for me by telling me what I should think, feel, and do. I discovered that I do not need to do what others tell me to do.

When I started this round of therapy, I was not fully aware of what was going on. I was too heavily medicated. I was very anxious. My memory of this time is spotty, but I remember my therapist teaching me how to ease my own anxieties.

Next there was a point where it was necessary to change my medications. She helped me with ideas about how to do that safely and with medical guidance. Then there was a time when therapy should end. I felt I was being "weaned," and I felt quite ready for that. These stages occurred over a period of about eighteen months. Part of the time I lived in her area for two or three months at a time, and part of the time I returned to my own home town.

As a result of encouragement to listen to myself, and to do what I believe is right for me, I found an indisputable medical source of information about my medication, Lithium. I adjusted the amount of my medication, regained most of my memory without losing the effects of the Lithium, and returned to work.

Barbara's story raises many questions for the therapist who is not medically trained. We believe that medications are sometimes helpful and necessary, and sometimes unnecessary. We will not treat anyone who is manic-depressive who is not taking Lithium (or one of the more recently discovered drugs) with medical supervision. However, we frequently encounter people who are so heavily medicated that they cannot function.

We advise people to take responsibility for themselves by working with physicians who are careful not to over-medicate them. When Barbara came to see me the second time she was so heavily medicated she could hardly function. She could not safely drive, lost her way almost daily, and was highly confused. In time, though, she was able to establish the optimum dosage for herself. At the same time, she established that she did not need to take the additional anti-depressant she had been given originally.

GRACE

When I came into my office, Grace was standing there looking like a sleek race horse waiting at the gate for the race to start. Racing was her life. Waiting was not her forte. She began talking even before we were seated and she continued such a volley of chatter that I quickly said, "Stop. Put your feet comfortably on the floor, you arms on your chair, and take some deep breaths. Now, tell me your story."

Grace had no idea how fast her life was racing. When she finally quieted herself, she told me that she was utterly exhausted, tired of struggling, and then she began sobbing out her pain and suffering. Grace had come to see me as a kind of last resort, hoping that finally she could understand why things were in such a mess and exchange her confusion and tears for "meaning, purpose, and peace."

Grace's Story

My adult life began when I became pregnant at age seventeen and my lover and I were forced to leave our Catholic high school. We got married and began to "play house." Our baby girl was born in

1971, and six weeks later I was pregnant again. Another baby arrived in 1972, but eighteen months later my marriage was finished.

For the next ten years I searched for meaning, purpose, and peace. My search led me through alcohol and drug abuse, countless sexual affairs, a second marriage, frantic entertaining, excessive and compulsive eating, returning to college, and a string of jobs. I was very depressed and often immobilized by the "black mood." When I had energy, I was scattered, "charged up," or "zooming."

When I was about thirty I had an especially difficult time. My second marriage was falling apart and I was in love with another man. Within one week I actually considered three different careers, and finally realized how confused I was. I was out of control and felt as if I were living two lives; alienated from one, unsure of the other.

A psychologist named Barbara thought she could help me to understand myself and to find some relief from my emotional pain. I learned a number of helpful things from her, but I kept fluctuating between having a sense of well-being and being miserable. When I was earning money I felt OK, but I would soon find an excuse to quit my job and return to my hometown with the unconscious hope that my lover and I would live together and I would be taken care of. I thought I wanted freedom, but on an emotional level, I was afraid to be alone. My mood swings were not quite as intense as they had been before therapy, but I still had bouts of rage and self-pity, on top of chronic depression. My sense of well-being was contingent on externals: my lover, my job, money. I felt victimized—not responsible for my own unhappiness.

I began reading the Bible, moved into the home of a wealthy friend, stopped working, squandered my savings, consulted a Chinese acupuncturist, an astrologer, and a psychic, enrolled in a culinary school, and then returned to college. I attended A.C.O.A. (Adult Children of Alcoholics) meetings. I bought "new-age" visualization tapes and starting reading about myths and goddesses. I was still depressed, confused, needy, frightened, filled with guilt, and very angry.

After a terrible period of depression, I was referred to Ruth by a friend. Later on I was in group therapy with Dawn. Three things made the difference between my earlier therapy and my therapy with these two women. First, I was more aware of myself and what I needed to change. Second, both Ruth and Dawn brought a creative and loving approach to their sessions. My gut feeling let me know that I crossed the paths of two very "special" women and I was excited by their wisdom and the graceful and enthusiastic way in which they lived their own lives. Second, I was offered information, practical applications of therapeutic skills, and loving kindness. In my previous therapy I had been the patient in a chair across the desk from a clinician who seemed very remote.

Now I was offered many tools for solving my own problems. First, an introduction to Transactional Analysis (T.A.), which taught me how to heal my inner Child by visualizing a loving Parent who gave me reassuring messages. I did pillow work, that is, I held a pillow (later a teddy bear), pretending that this was the inner Child. While I patted the pillow or the bear I gave myself loving strokes such as "You are a precious child," "You are the daughter I have always wanted," I will take care of you forever." "It's OK to ask for what you want. If I can't give it to you, I'll tell you why." This reparenting is a very effective tool. The power it imparts comes slowly, but after several months I just knew I could take care of myself for the rest of my life. To this day, I take the first moments in the morning to hold my bear and tell myself how much I love my inner Child. Through this reparenting technique, I found enormous strength and courage because I faced the demons of my fear, anger, and depression.

Secondly, I was taught how to release old anger. I had the idea that the only way to deal with anger was by direct confrontation. Since I was afraid to do this very often, I just pushed down anger for years. In therapy I learned safe ways to deal with that repressed anger: 1) beating a pillow or having a temper tantrum in the privacy of my car or bedroom, 2) writing out my anger in the journal I kept, 3) yelling at the negative voices that screamed in my ears. Each of these things helped, but what was most healing was when I replaced the old destructive negative messages with positive, loving messages and experiences. I visualized safe places and situations where I could retreat and in meditation renew myself with love and acceptance. Sometimes, pretending I was one of my parents, I would write a loving letter to myself. By doing all of these things, I gradually realized my own power as a woman and autonomous person.

When I realized that I had the power to change myself, my therapist taught me other things. Important among them was how to solve problems. She taught me to look at all my options for solving a particular problem, then to test each option, and finally to choose the best solution among those options. I found out that there are no magical ways to solve problems, but clear thinking and awareness of feelings pave the way to good solutions. I had never had this kind of loving parenting before and it gave me enormous freedom to find my own way rather than being overwhelmed by decision making. I also learned to have a back-up plan if my first solution didn't work. This took away a lot of anxiety.

In addition to effective problem solving I learned to take charge of my depression by knowing that it was anger turned in on myself. When I was angry I would say, "I will not turn this anger inward." Then I would write in my journal, repeating this phrase over and over. Finally I would replace the anger with love and kindness by using my reparenting technique.

When I had enough courage, I tackled "my father pain and my mother anger." My father and I had been in conflict for as long as I could remember, and my mother had been the peacemaker. I had repressed pain, anger, and fear since I was a child because I had felt emotionally abandoned. I was never physically abused, hungry, or without a home, but I was very lonely. In my early years I had just raw opposition to my parents: unbridled anger and resentment flung at them every chance I could. In therapy I made a startling discovery. One time I expressed bitter emotion when I remembered how my father had been kind to me. I realized I had to find out where that pain came from. The image I had was that I had a ball of string that wound around my father, my mother, and my lover (who was a kind of father figure). I finally unraveled the mysterious ball. I realized that my parents had done the best they could because they too carried pain from their childhoods. When I realized this, I became more accepting of them and we now enjoy better relations with one another.

After I had been in individual therapy, I went to group therapy because I knew that group would provide a safe place for me to explore myself in the presence of others. I was afraid to try group, but I decided to take the risk. Group was a safe place. I learned to ask for what I wanted. My Child was accepted and loved and my Parent learned to be kind yet firm. I was able to show my sadness, loneliness, fear, and anger in front of other people and replace the old negative feelings with healthy ones.

For many years, I had struggled to work out my own understanding of God and religion. My magical Child used to think that God took care of everything and that I had no responsibility. Then I thought I had to do it all and God wasn't important at all. Now I believe that there is a balance between God's providence and my personal responsibility. God will always provide everything I need, but I may not always get everything I want.

Through therapy I have found compassion and understanding for myself and for other people. Therapy has helped me find and name my wounds, and then given me the bandages and ointments I need to heal those wounds. My journey in therapy was a spiral, bringing me back to where I have always been, but moving upward. Today when I awaken, I give praise and thanksgiving for what has been and for what is to come. Therapy has given me the opportunity to become a very grateful person.

Grace always thought there was something wrong with her, but also knew that if she were desperate someone would look after her. The youngest of three children, she learned early in life that she was supposed to be helpless and adorable. She was not happy in this position, but had no idea how to change.

As an adult who had never grown up, she became a constant seeker who never found what she wanted. She knew there had to be answers somewhere as she tried drugs, magical and mystical solutions, and searching for "the right man." She vacillated between being charming and helpless and being rebellious. She would have exciting ideas for earning money and would then work an eighty-hour week, or she would be disillusioned and not work at all or know what she wanted to do. When all else failed, she realized she needed to do something for herself.

She began therapy with us and during this time a wonderful thing happened. Two significant people in her life refused to play "rescuer" any longer. This meant that she had to grow up, to take care of herself and solve her problems, or look for new "rescuers." With her added strength and resolve, she decided to grow up. She has embarked upon a career which uses her talents and creativity and also provides her with the means to support herself. She likes her new lifestyle more than being the perpetual little girl.

MEGAN

Megan appeared to be out of place in our stress management group. Unusually pretty, seemingly whole and well-adjusted, she was envied by all the other women who were admittedly struggling with their marriages, their relationships with their children, and their lack of self-confidence.

Megan's Prince Charming had come and taken her to his castle, where she said she was living happily. The problem was that her Prince had turned out to be a frog, and Megan was back in rags, sweeping the hearth and mothering her five children. She was also like the "old woman who lived in the shoe and had so many children she didn't know what to do." Megan kept herself going by living in a dream world, pretending to herself and to everyone else that she was just fine.

Megan's Story

I came into therapy after having gone to a "stress management" group. I had thought a group in stress management would be interesting, but I didn't think that I needed it for myself. I was handling my life just fine. Curiosity and fascination with the leader were my real motivations for signing up for the group. At the end of the group, I knew I needed therapy and needed it badly.

The reason I had not been conscious of my problems was that I had lived my life as a heroine and survivor, able to deal with whatever came my way. In reality this wasn't true. I had denied my own needs physically, emotionally, and spiritually. I had stuffed away my despair and resignation behind a facade of looking good. I had fooled a lot of people this way, including myself. I looked like the ideal "Mom," the ideal wife.

I remember in the first session of "stress management," the leader, who later became my therapist, asked every person in the room to introduce themselves by telling the group something about themselves. I thought to myself, "I don't need to be here with these 'wimpy, soap-opera' women." (Years later, I realized in my own drama, I was the "Queen Mother.") When my turn came I said, "I'm Megan and I'm married to Ted, I'm the mother of four children and pregnant with my fifth." I thought this was my identity. The leader said, "Wife and mother, but who are you?" The question was asked very kindly, but I had no idea who I was outside of my relationship with my husband and children. In that moment an opening was created in my life which has never closed. I saw how narrow and limited I was. I had no identity. My life was lived exclusively through others. My family and my cultural and religious upbringing told me that was how it should be. I was supposed to be selfless (presumed to be the antithesis of selfish). For me being selfless meant the absence of Self, of being a person in myself. Selfless had meant not life, but death. I was controlled by what others thought of me, and I was therefore completely at the mercy of all the "shoulds." "You should suffer. You should give everything to your husband and children, not yourself. You should work until you're exhausted." I was at everyone's mercy and I was therefore a victim of the whims of fate.

No wonder I was so unhappy, although I wouldn't admit it. "Is this all there is to life? There must be something more. I thought I was going to make a contribution to the world. I give up. I can't do anything to make a real impact. My life is without meaning." Thoughts such as these kept running through my head although I wasn't willing to look at their meaning.

My therapist asked what fairy tale had been my favorite as a child, and with whom I had identified in that story. I immediately knew I was Cinderella. As a child, a friend had once asked me if I were Cinderella, since I had to do so much of the work at home. Of course I was, and I honestly thought that one day the Prince would come, whisk me out of the ashes forever, and take me to a glorious land of riches and glamor. "So, did you marry the Prince?" the therapist asked. Without any hesitation I said yes. Then it came to me. I was still in the ashes. My married life had always been one of lack, struggle, and crisis—never any money, never the right job for Ted, never the right town. We were gypsies. Where we were or what we were doing was never it. "This isn't it; this isn't it."

My relationship with my husband was not an honest relationship. I remember, after the birth of my first child, thinking to myself, "Who the heck is this guy? What have I done? We are no more compatible than oil and water." I talked easily, Ted didn't. I could never find out what he was thinking or feeling. By the time I met Ruth and Dawn, I had accepted that all this was what I had to live with. When I was a child, I had seen only two possibilities for my life. One, go to college because "Daddy" said so, or two, marry the Prince who would take care of me so that I would live happily ever after. In both cases, I was not taking responsibility for my own life. I wanted "Daddy" to decide or my Prince to come. It seemed easier to marry the Prince.

When we first married, I thought Ted and I were intimate because we had sexual relations often and then had five children. When I became aware of problems in our marriage, I thought it must be my fault. After all, Ted was faithful, didn't go to bars, and worked hard for his family. What more could anyone want?

When I was honest with myself, I knew that I wanted a love partner, someone to talk to deeply, someone who would be honest with me and not just try to placate me and smooth over situations. I wanted to have fun and laughter. But in reality we had a mess. Instead of an adventure, life was a struggle. Before I decided to have therapy I was completely confused, very unhappy, and superficially resigned to my fate.

In addition to my unhappiness about my marriage, I had a second problem: an almost constant state of feeling overwhelmed. In my life as a child I had learned that it was my job to handle everything at an age when I was far too young for the responsibility. I was the oldest child in an alcoholic family. I was mother to my brothers and both parents. I thought I could survive anything life brought on. Never knowing my own limitations, I lived with crisis and overwhelming circumstances. I was under continual stress and seemed unable ever to "take it easy." What I heard people say fed my ego. "Isn't she wonderful? She has five kids. Her husband's never home. She never has any money, but somehow she manages. How does she do it?" I didn't know how unhappy I was.

Scenarios of escape were constantly going through my head. "Maybe Ted will die suddenly. Then I'll be the noble widow. Maybe we'll move to New Zealand and everything will be all right." The thoughts about Ted's death really scared me and I thought that I was a weirdo or perhaps mentally ill. I wanted out of my marriage, but that seemed not a choice.

The mask did not work. I could fool others but not myself. The denial did not work. Living in a commune had not solved my problems. Neither did marijuana. Even the people who constantly rescued me did not make me really happy. I grew tired of being a martyr.

I was in private therapy and later in group therapy with both Ruth and Dawn. I learned that if I really wanted to have the life I said I wanted I could make responsible choices to direct my future. I could choose to go on being a "victim" or a creator of my own happiness. I could play out the old script from my childhood—Cinderella—or I could put a new show on the road. I had a choice between honoring myself and using my abilities or being a peon living in servitude to others.

My therapists gave me permission to take care of myself by becoming my own nurturing mother and loving the little Child within me. They modeled this behavior in their own lives, and I liked what I saw. I learned to rest after I had worked a reasonable amount. I gave myself permission to take myself out to lunch or dinner. I learned to take care of my appearance. All these ideas had been alien to me because I thought a mother must give every-thing to her children. Now I realized that by taking care of myself I was better able to take care of my family. (Who needs a worn-out bedraggled, angry, suffering mother?)

It has been seven years since I finished therapy and I'm still growing. My children now see me taking care of myself and be-coming a real person. This teaches them how to love and to care for themselves. Now I love and honor my godliness. I know that true love and forgiveness for others must begin with our love and forgiveness of ourselves. Our love comes from the God within us. My children have a happy, alive, and enthusiastic Mom to be with. And I have a happy and enthusiastic Child within me. I love my own inner Child. I love the good mother I have become.

Megan was a good example of what has been called a "Res-cuer," i.e., a person who takes care of other people as a way of hiding from themselves their own desperate need to be cared for. Megan's real position in the Drama Triangle (see page 136) was that of "Victim," that is, a person whose suffering seems to have come about because of circumstances beyond her control. Megan was always in a crisis situation which elicited help and sympathy from tender-hearted people who thought that all she needed was a little something now. The trouble was that very quickly after the problem of the moment was solved, Megan found herself in an-other crisis. The cycle repeated again and again.

It took many sessions of therapy for Megan to see that she brought most of the crises on herself by not using her thinking abilities to solve her problems, thereby adding new woes to her already existing suffering. She kept on "rescuing" her Peter Pan husband, but her solutions were not realistic or mature because she saw herself as incapable of finding practical solutions—only stopgap measures. When Megan had the courage to face her real position, an inner Child "Victim," she stopped playing "Big Mommy" Parent and began to deal realistically with her own needs and those of her five children. She became a successful business-woman, took care of her own needs and those of her children, and separated from her sixth child (husband Ted), since Ted wanted to go on playing Peter Pan.

STEPHEN

When Stephen called for an appointment, I was surprised. I had been seeing his colleague Don for some time and had met Stephen, but I had no thought of Stephen's needing therapy. He was one of the hidden ones. No one would have guessed Stephen's story and this was just what Stephen wanted. He was a very competent professional, had carried major responsibility in a large city corporation, had gone to the best schools, was extremely personable, handsome, intelligent, and seemingly well adjusted. Stephen was admired, sought after, and envied.

The problem was that Stephen knew there was more to life than outer appearances and achievements. He knew that self-acceptance, purpose, meaning, and inner peace were absolutely essential to quality of life. Quite interestingly, however, when he came for his first session he presented his persona. He came in appearing as competent and easy as he had appeared to so many people for so long and he even had an air of defiance about him, almost daring me to discover his secrets.

When I made it clear to him that here in these sessions he did not need to pretend, to compete, to meet anyone else's standards, to be anything other than himself, Stephen trusted enough gradually to begin to show his deep wounds, his childhood scars, his early tears. Stephen describes this period as "mongrel," barbarian," "sniffy."

Stephen's Story

I first came into therapy because a friend of mine was in it and he suggested that I go also. I could tell that he was getting a great deal out of his therapy and I wanted the same thing. I was in a great deal of emotional pain and anguish and I wanted to feel better and to be more mentally healthy.

There were many problems I needed help with: sex, death, purpose and meaning in life, church, God, career, family. They all seemed overwhelming. Some years earlier, while I was in graduate school, I had seen a psychiatrist for about six months. Along with my weekly appointments, he had prescribed Valium to help my depression. I tried keeping busy just to fill time so that I didn't have to think about my problems. When I was especially depressed, I would sleep an inordinate amount of time. I took many self-help, personal enrichment, and other courses as a way to solve my problems, and I prayed to God for deliverance, but the problems remained.

When I began therapy with you, I could immediately see the difference from the therapy I had had with the psychiatrist. Instead of prescribing medication, I was shown how to take charge of myself and begin to solve my problems. I was given practical tools for dealing with my behavior and my actions and reactions to other people. I was given responsibility for my own mental health and destiny. I was treated as an adult and not patronized as sick or helpless. This therapy was different in that I felt I had the first opportunity to tell my whole story, that someone was actually listening to me and understood what I was trying to say.

I learned many things. Most important, I learned that no matter what I said, did, thought, or had done, I was OK. This meant I could own my own thoughts and feelings and know that they were real for me. I learned not to project my own thoughts and feelings onto others, but if I did project I was aware of what I was doing. I found out that everyone has a sex life and we must all make decisions about how we live ours. I discovered that it was OK for me to be angry, and to express that anger appropriately so I would not hurt myself or others. I began to take my own life and problems less seriously, to be more sensitive to other people, and to recognize their problems too.

To find out that I am not physically ugly, that I am a loving and kind person, was wonderful. I learned to think on my feet and to ask for what I want. I found out that I had always been a "pleaser" and that adapted behavior had kept me from being myself and taking care of myself. The tools I gained in therapy enabled me not only to begin to solve the problems I had, but would help me for the rest of my life.

Looking back on all of this, I think of my therapy in five stages: 1) "Mongrel-Barbarian"—Describes my feelings before therapy. I felt disjointed, not together, going in all directions, unfocused like the uncivilized masses in the jungle, wandering aimlessly with no true sense of purpose or awareness of self—struggling, struggling. 2) "Sniffing"—An inquisitive phase—testing the "therapeutic waters" to see if they could be trusted and that I would be safe in therapy. This phase also included "shocking" the therapist to see if she could cope with the realities of my life and accept who I was. 3) "Student/Education/Neophyte"—A period of dealing with very personal problems, reading material in Transactional Analysis and Jungian analysis, and listening to what my therapist thought about all this. 4) "Apprenticeship"—A long period of applying new-found knowledge, and practice in using it. This phase also included group therapy. 5) "Master"—The Apprentice became his own Master. I no longer needed therapy and I terminated it, grateful to the therapist, but ready to move out on my own.

The changes in my life were not immediate, but they were nonetheless significant, even radical. As a result of my therapy, I changed my entire outlook on life, changed careers, married, and had a child. I took control of my life and no longer merely reacted to it. Now I am living!

For many reasons children sometimes make early decisions not to marry later in life. Often these are tragic decisions because they keep people from the joy of living a happy life with a chosen partner. Stephen had made such a decision when he was very young. Interestingly, women found him handsome and attractive, but he blocked out their attention and told himself he was ugly. About a year after he finished therapy, Stephen moved to another community where he became the pastor of a church. There he found a woman who loved him for himself. Stephen no longer needed to be defensive with her. They married and had a child, and Stephen now knows that he can be himself—husband, father, clergyman, Stephen.

Marital Conflict

AMY

After a talk I had given in a midwestern town, John asked about my weekend workshops. Two months later, he enrolled himself and his wife Amy. I soon realized Amy had come because she was a dutiful wife and was used to doing what she was told. All that weekend she was hidden in John's shadow. He was charming, handsome, very successful in business, and quite used to captivating the ladies. Amy, on the other hand, was quiet, plain, and seldom noticed.

Some weeks later Amy called for a private therapy session. I was both surprised and delighted. Perhaps, I thought, this call is a glimmer of hope for Amy's tomorrows. But when Amy came for her first session, everything about her let me know that she expected me to tell her what do to. I was, in her eyes, the wise doctor. She was the helpless patient. Amy writes about our first session.

From that time on I knew that with support and encouragement she would find her own way. The universe is always on the side of healing, health, and wholeness, and often a person needs to be told this by another whom they respect. This information gives a kind of permission for moving out of destructive patterns and into healthier behavior. Amy is a good example of how a person hears the good news of life, believes it because she is ready to hear, and then moves quickly forward. She seemed to devour every bit of teaching and information we discussed. She seemed eager to try on every new behavior she discovered. She left each session with new insight and plans for changing small or sometimes major things in her life. She returned with experiences which then became the learning material for the next session. She made mistakes, of course. She stumbled. She fell, but she got up and went on. Perhaps because she had been so beaten down, her new self began to rise up so beautifully. Amy was becoming a genuine person.

Amy's Story

My husband wanted me to change, and I came into therapy to please him. I didn't disagree with him that I needed "fixing," but it had never occurred to me to have therapy just for myself. All my life I had a shame-based self-image and such low self-esteem that I was drawn into all kinds of dysfunctional relationships, first with my parents and then with my husband and my children. I had never separated emotionally from my parents, and since our family had been so enmeshed and closed I had recreated that same pattern in my marriage. I had decided that there must be something seriously wrong with me, and so I spent most of my time trying to please other people.

I had tried self help by reading magazines and taking quizzes in articles with titles such as "Are You Ruining Your Marriage?" or "Are You Making Your Husband Happy?" My focus was always on what I was doing to make things go wrong.

My husband decided we should go to a weekend workshop on Transactional Analysis. During the hundred-mile drive from our home, he told me he was having an affair with a younger woman and wanted a separation. Interestingly enough, he did not ask for a divorce. I was so depressed and tearful during that entire weekend that I could only focus on my failure as a wife-person. I honestly didn't know the difference between a wife and an individual person. At the close of the weekend, the therapist who was the leader came over to me, looked straight into my eyes, and with great care and compassion said, "I am concerned about you, Amy. Keep yourself safe and do something good for *you*." No one had ever before given me permission to care about myself and to consider "Me." Shortly after that weekend, my husband moved out of state, and the emotion and pain that I felt motivated me to do something. I called the therapist who had led the weekend and made an appointment. I should add that the weekend had not been a weekend for treatment, but a time to understand the framework, language, and concepts of Transactional Analysis.

My first session of therapy was very significant because it set the tone for my entire future. The therapist treated me differently from anyone I had ever been with. Let me tell you what happened.

When I arrived for my appointment on a lovely summer day we met in an outside summer house office. After a brief moment of re-introduction, the therapist asked me what I wanted from these sessions. I don't know exactly what I answered, but I do know that I communicated this message, "Well, you tell me what I need." In other words, "Fix me" was my attitude and my approach. The therapist's response was, "It's important that you tell me what *you* want to accomplish, and I will help you find some ways to do that."

There was a long period of silence. I had no intention of answering. After some time, the therapist picked up a book and started to read to herself. I was furious. First I thought, "There is something wrong with me. I'm not doing this right. What does she want?" Next, I felt my anger boil up, and I said, "I just drove a hundred miles, and I have to drive a hundred miles home again. I'm paying all this money to you, and I had to hire a baby-sitter." I got angrier and angrier. The therapist said nothing. I don't know how much time passed. It seemed forever, but it was probably four or five minutes. Then I said, "I don't like that you're reading." She put down her book and in a very quiet voice said, "This is your time, and we can spend it any way you want to. But you need to take charge and decide what you want."

Then, with great difficulty, I began taking responsibility for my therapy. I established some goals, and ended the session feeling hopeful and empowered. I am convinced that had I not had that experience I would never have gone back to therapy. I had asked to be told what to do, but I would have been furious if she had told me. Instead I was given the freedom to find out what I wanted and to "go for it."

I continued to work in therapy over many months. I lessened my emotional pain and sense of abandonment. I had a few meetings during that time with my husband, to try for reconciliation. This was counter-productive to my therapy, however, because I would enter the old dysfunctional system although I didn't even realize it at that time. But my growth in therapy was so effective that it was a positive and powerful force despite those meetings with my husband.

After a few months, my husband and I reconciled, even though I briefly resisted because I was getting healthier and beginning to explore some options for myself. Very soon after our reconciliation, however, I regressed into my old patterns with John the dominant and "superior" one.

More therapy and then the therapist introduced me to the concepts of Carl Jung. I was immediately drawn to his work, and began to record my dreams, take them to my sessions, and understand how my unconscious was speaking to me through my dreams. I had started with Transactional Analysis, which focuses on outward problems. Now I was being led to focus inwardly and internally. The dream analysis took me into a major new development and brought me closer to my goal of self-actualization and individualization. This important level of work has continued ever since. I find that I am living more introspectively and connecting with feelings of joy which I had known earlier in life as a child and a young woman.

Today I know that I am important. I am a human being with a soul and a purpose. Now I share myself with other people and give some of the "goodness of me" back to others. Knowing this, I made a professional change and finally became a therapist myself. This was a long road, since I had not been to college. After several years, I finished my undergraduate work and then earned a Master's degree in counseling with special concentration in addiction counseling.

In my therapy, I developed a wholistic attitude toward life. I learned not to somatize my tensions and anxieties, and I have become healthier physically, emotionally, intellectually, and spiritually. My therapist was a role model for me, and through her modeling, I learned to move toward my goals, respond to other people in more healthy ways and live inside myself with care and love.

When Amy began college, she was supporting two teenage children and had limited financial resources. But she was determined to get a college degree and soon evidenced her industry, discipline, and intellectual capability. When she began her graduate training in counseling psychology, I knew that she would one day become an excellent professional therapist. She has become just that. Amy, who hid in John's shadow, has become Amy who lives in the sunlight of her own inner beauty and wholeness. She says she has received wonderful insights from her own therapy sessions. She now gives much to those who come to her for healing and wholeness.

ELIZABETH

Elizabeth was shaking when she first came to see me. Although she was in her middle twenties she looked and sounded like a little girl who had done something very bad and had been sent to her room to wait for her punishment. The longer she was there, and the more she thought about what she had done, the worse she felt. She had no fear that anyone would hurt her physically. It was much worse than that: She felt as if no one would ever love her any more.

Elizabeth's Story

I was getting a divorce and was unable to sleep, because of preoccupation with what people—especially my family— would think.

No one in our church or family had ever been divorced. Good doctors were surely not divorced! Divorce was only for harlots and other "bad" people. I felt shut off from every support system I had. I was acting in a way not considered appropriate by my family, church, or medical school community. At least I felt divorce was not acceptable and could not be discussed openly in those circles.

I was referred to my therapist through the Women's Crisis line; I was reaching out from my usual contacts. I'd had no previous therapy. I did not consider medication. I endured my anxiety alone until I called the crisis line.

I learned a lot of wonderful things in therapy. For one thing, I learned how to approach problems like anxiety by asking questions such as, "What is the worst thing that could happen?" and, "How could you deal with that?" I found I could think about what I was feeling, and then it did not seem so overwhelming. I learned how to sort out feelings and label them "mad," "sad," "scared," and "glad." I discovered that nobody makes me feel anything, and I cannot make anyone else feel anything if they are not willing to feel that way. I began to own responsibility for how I feel and act, and came to realize I cannot make others do bad or good things. I also learned stoppers of certain behaviors. Now I stop pressuring myself to hurry up (and generally make mistakes) by reminding myself, "There's time enough to do it right."

Group therapy was particularly good to help me realize that I was raised well and my problems were no greater than other people's problems. In group I also learned many useful ways of taking care of myself—strokes, getting a massage, soaking in the tub after a day's work, each of which is good preventive medicine.

My first visit significantly lowered my anxiety level. That by itself was enough to get me through the next few weeks. I think after that, learning about Parent voices and Child needs helped me to sort out many things. Acting out those voices helped me to realize how real they were. I learned how I was scaring myself and making myself anxious.

As the initial crisis eased, a deeper level of insecurity about being loved became apparent to me. I had an initial resolution to that problem, a wonderfully therapeutic group rock that I still remember. Some re-parenting messages were implanted then. At times I feel a definite need for reinforcement of those messages. I'd often felt there was something wrong because no one ever seemed to tell me I was pretty. In group therapy I heard that and believed it. After that I gave more attention to my appearance and many people found me attractive.

I learned a lot of preventive medicine for feeling down or depressed—what strokes are, how to get them, and give them to myself. These things still help me daily to resolve stress and seek the comfort I need. Finally, I began to learn the techniques to use to start others on their own way to sorting out their problems. I decided to become Board Certified in Preventive Medicine!

I think my therapist's method, and in particular her asking the questions that bring answers from the patient, is very good. In this way, one learns what questions to ask oneself when a problem arises. Also, it is hard to denounce the answers since they come from the Self.

As a result of my therapy I got over my anxiety about my divorce and was able to remove parental and societal negative statements from my inner Parent voices. I have, as a result, been able to move more confidently through life without that historical event dragging me down.

My knowledge of T.A. theory, and other information I received in therapy has helped me sort out many difficult situations with emergency department patients.

I have been more positive about myself and as a result less compulsive than I would have been otherwise. I am still quite achievement–oriented, having become Board Certified in two specialties, but I had lots of good times in the process.

I am less "shy" than I used to be. I meet people more easily in settings other than work, because I worry less about what other people think.

Looking back at myself, I see that anxiety was much of my problem. Depression and sadness were underlying my anxiety, and anger was over it. Since I have known how to deal with that, I have had the skills to get through some tough times involving miscarriages, criticism from nurses, and patients who have died. Now, I am taking some time away from work to care for and enjoy my first child.

In addition to her anxiety and guilt over her divorce, Elizabeth also pressured herself. She did this by convincing herself, in her own head, that she was supposed to be perfect and please everybody else. Whenever she did not do both of those things, she put extra pressure on herself by hurrying up to try to fix things. When she did that, she became harried and agitated. Elizabeth's main work was learning to take time to think things through, and to stop pressuring herself unduly.

She grew to accept herself. She gave herself permission to do her best, rather than striving for perfection. And she came to find that the whole world did not fall apart when she did not please everyone else all of the time.

GARY

Gary looked like a college football star. He had graduated some years ago, but every kid in the neighborhood knew Gary had been a well-known quarterback. He loved kids, and he told me the first time I saw him that he felt like a kid himself. His own children adored him. Gary had "made it big" in business at a very young age, and money was no problem for him. His investments were excellent, and he was to all outward appearances a very happy yuppie. Why then had this man come to see me? One thing was terribly wrong—his marriage was "yucky." Since Gary was fun-loving, hard working, intelligent, and well-liked, how had he chosen a woman who was so unsuited to him? I soon discovered that, odd as it may seem, he had chosen a wife who treated him just as his father had treated him from the time he was little until the present. Since he worked for his father's company, this presented quite a problem.

Therapists often see a strange phenomenon that they call living in one's "script." Children learn from their parents and other significant adults what to do and how to do it, what's important in life, and what values to incorporate. Are they to grow up being winners or losers, successes or failures, happy people or endurers, leaders or followers? If parents model destructive behaviors, values, and life patterns, children will often adopt these same models for themselves. Alcoholic parents usually produce dysfunctional children. Depressed and angry parents produce children who are overwhelmed by depression and anger. On the other hand, if parents model healthy lifestyles, children will often adopt healthy ways of living. By the time a child is six to eight years old, he will usually have made major decisions about how he is going to live his own life. These decisions are made in his unconscious and are, of course, based on insufficient information, i.e., his six-year-old world. He believes that what he experiences is the way life is. In later years, even if his lifestyle and attitudes bring about pain and failure, he will continue in those attitudes and behaviors because he is familiar and comfortable with what he is used to. When, as an adult, he sees other lifestyles which seem to bring about more happiness and success, he will think he is unable to change himself and unable to do anything about his own suffering.

This was what had happened to Gary. Metaphorically speaking, he had married his father. When he was a child, Gary had believed that if he were a good and obedient little boy his father would really love him. Now, if he were obedient and good enough, his wife would really love him. He saw her as rigid, demanding, overly serious, and always nagging. Perhaps he could get her to stop nagging and love him for himself. It didn't work. She knew what was best and how he should be, and she was going to see that happen.

Before me sat the football hero and yuppie executive. Before me sat the little boy who could never "do it right" for daddy or Clara. Before me sat the little boy who was sick of trying. Gary was getting ready to grow up.

Gary's Story

My wife and I were having serious problems that we couldn't handle at all: sexual problems, problems with communication, and the basic problem that we had grown to dislike and distrust each other. We trusted each other's fidelity, but neither of us trusted what the other said about anything. It was the epitome of communication breakdown. At the same time we were trying to rekindle a burned-out fire.

For me the most pressing of these problems was the sexual one. I wanted sex and she didn't. She could "live her life without it," as she expressed it. Not me. Toward the end, I was willing to try anything to respark the fire, although honestly there hadn't been much fire on her part from the start. She had pretty well convinced me that sex more often than once a month and anywhere else than in bed was sick. I was pretty well sure that I was sick and perverted.

We decided to persevere and endure. We had, or at least I had, resolved that we would stay married for as long as we could for the sake of the kids.

It took a long time for me to decide I would get some help. When I started therapy I didn't know how to begin or what to do. I only knew I felt lousy and wanted to feel better and get on with my life.

The most valuable thing I learned in therapy was that I didn't have to take Clara's abuse any more. I found out that I had subjected myself to the same kind of abuse in my relationship with my father, and before I could cope with the problems with my wife, I was going to have to deal once and for all with the stuff buried deep within me surrounding my relationship with my dad. When I had done that, I learned that I could take charge of my own life by deciding to stop letting other people run it for me.

The first part of therapy was what I would call the "recognition stage." I had to come to grips with the real skeletons in my closet. Second, I had to resolve the inner conflicts: Who's in charge? What do I owe to myself? What will happen if I say no when someone wants me to say yes? Finally, I had to act on what I discovered about myself, namely, that I could regain control of my own life and stop letting everybody dump on me.

When I finished therapy, I changed my life for the better. I divorced Clara, resolved my conflicts with my dad, took a new job, took charge of myself, and then I married the woman of my dreams! I expect "to live happily ever after."

Little needs to be said other than to comment on Gary's courage and discipline. It is not easy for most men to admit that they have problems or to talk about their pain, especially not easy for men who have "made it." Gary worked hard, and went straight for the goal post. He married a lovely woman, and they now have the marriage they both deserve.

HEATHER

Heather was the ideal Southern lady, refined, soft-spoken, immaculately groomed, sweetly dressed. I had met her mother and her aunt before Heather called, and Heather looked exactly as I had expected her to look. I think she was just what her grandmother would have expected her to be also.

Whatever Heather had experienced in her childhood, adolescence, and young womanhood was carefully cloaked beneath her crisp cotton frock, white stockings, and spotless pink shoes. She was almost ashamed to tell me why she had come. Like a child, she felt bewildered by how all "this" could have happened to a faithful wife and caring mother. Heather had been told that if she followed the teachings of her parents, her social class, and her church, she would one day marry, have lovely children, and live happily ever after. She had been indeed a Sleeping Beauty: One day, just as she believed, her Prince had come and carried her off to married bliss.

No one had prepared her for a husband who lived in a little boy's world where he thought he was a prince. Whatever he wanted he had been given as a child, and now he thought he should still have his way. He lied to his "mommy" (wife) and hid his secret mistress in a cozy apartment. Heather had watched television and read books about sordid marriages, but bad things didn't happen to good little girls. No wonder she felt ashamed and guilty as if everything were somehow her fault.

It took many sessions of therapy for Heather to learn that although she had had a loving mother and father, they had taught her what they believed and had not wanted her to know about "the other side." They had wanted to protect her from all that. Without loving her parents less, Heather gradually was able to grow up, face the depth of her own agony, and establish a set of truths and values that were her own, not just the mirror of values of those in authority. For two years, as she kept growing in her own maturity, she hoped that her husband would value his marriage and children enough to give up his Peter Pan life and become a mature husband and father. For a moment, it looked as if this could happen. I saw Carl a few times by himself and a few times with Heather as we tried to work things through. It became clear, however, that according to Carl all the problems in the marriage were Heather's fault. I had met many Carls before in my practice—the eternal little boys who were often "character disorders"—charming, handsome, making fools out of others, lying even to themselves, and having no real desire to change themselves.

Heather saw that she must focus on her own growth and maturity and not wait for her Prince to make her happy. She did just that. Step by step she saw how she had choices no matter what other people did. She could be frightened and sad or she could solve problems and find ways to be happy within herself and with her children.

Let Heather now tell you how she chose to get on with her life.

Heather's Story

For about twelve years I had been in a very rocky and unhappy marriage. My husband and I were incompatible and argued all the time. We couldn't agree on issues about money, sex, children, interests—anything. Many times I had suggested that we needed help to resolve our problems, but Carl was unwilling to go to see anyone since he felt he didn't need help. We had been on the brink of separation or divorce many times, but I could never go through with either.

I was extremely unsure of myself and was totally dominated by my husband. I always felt as if I could never measure up to his expectations. I knew we didn't belong together, but we had two small children and another baby on the way. I was a Catholic and for a very long time I did not consider divorce as an option. In the eighth month of my third pregnancy, I found out that my husband was having an affair. Even though we had had a horrible marriage, I was devastated. I felt this was the final insult.

I did summon enough courage to talk with him and ask him to end the affair so that we could try to salvage our marriage. I wanted to work things out, and so I began to examine how I might have failed in the marriage and how I could change. As I look back now, this affair had not caused the unhappiness in our marriage. But it did give me the push I needed to change my life.

When the youngest child was six weeks old, I was so miserable that I finally decided to enter therapy. After the first meeting I felt so much better knowing there was someone who would help me, but what I later learned helped me to help myself. My husband was very angry when I told him I had gone to see a therapist, and it was all I could do to return for a second appointment. Nonetheless, I decided to stick with it. I began going for sessions once a week, then twice a month, then monthly, then whenever I thought I needed to return. All along, I was gradually finding myself. Through the process of my therapy, I became a stronger person. I began to like myself and came to realize that I had a lot to offer. I realized I couldn't depend on myself or anyone else to make me happy; I had to do that for myself.

After two years Carl was still "playing house" with his mistress, still lying to me about it, and still believed that he had no problems. I finally realized that nothing had changed nor would it. I had given the marriage one last effort before I ended it, and now I knew it was the right decision to file for a divorce. I have never regretted that decision.

How did this happen—this change in me from being frightened, dependent, unsure and insecure to liking myself, knowing who I was, and what I needed to do? There were several steps in my therapy: 1) I examined exactly what the problems were in my life. 2) I looked at myself to find out why I had allowed things to occur the way they did in my life and let myself act the way I had acted. 3) I looked at my choices for problem-solving, and I chose the solutions I thought best. 4) I took the steps I needed to to change several things in my life.

As a result of my work in therapy, I became more independent of my husband, children, and parents. I took care of myself more lovingly and took responsibility for my own decisions. I stopped feeling guilty thinking I was neglecting my family when I did something for myself. I found a wonderful man to marry and I became a happy person.

I cannot say enough positive things about the value of therapy. I recommend it for everyone, not just those who have problems, but also those who want to grow and make things better in their lives.

About a year after she finished therapy Heather came back to see me. She had met a man she wanted to marry and who wanted to marry her. He too had had a broken marriage. In this case, Tom was the one who had tried to hold things together. Marion had no problems, so Tom had reluctantly filed for divorce. Now Heather and Tom wanted to begin a new life together. In their therapy sessions they had both become different people from the unwise teenagers they had been when they chose their spouses. Heather and Tom were not perfect. They had much growing to do, but they had learned from their past mistakes. They now knew how to work problems out as soon as they became aware of them. They are not only happily married, but they are together in their life goals and their commitment to maturity and wholeness.

JEAN

In her early forties, Jean was bright, highly intelligent, and impeccably groomed. She was aware of having been depressed and resentful for long periods, but that was not a major issue when she came. She knew she was angry most of the time and did not hesitate to show it. Her fuse was very short. She was not aware of how being angry was keeping her out of touch with her deep, dark fear—the fear of being abandoned, unloved, and unwanted.

Jean was an achiever and a super-responsible caretaker. She had excelled in her studies, she was an avid reader and connoisseur of the arts, and she was dedicated to helping others—especially children. At the same time she was hurting inside so much that she constantly clenched and unclenched her hands—not together, but separately. It was as if she were saying, "I'm struggling to hold on tight but there's nothing to cling to except my own hand."

Jean's Story

I came into therapy because my second marriage was in great difficulty. I had previously been married for fifteen years to a man who had become addicted to drugs and who had been consistently unfaithful; in addition, he handled anger by totally withdrawing and was quite able to live without speaking to me for months at a time. I had four children and had stayed in the marriage far too long, hoping against hope that I could "do things right" and get him to love me and treat me reasonably (I was no longer looking for "nicely" or "well." I was willing to settle for "reasonable").

After a long legal battle, I was divorced and met a man who was in the same profession as mine (I had gone back to school and gotten an advanced degree). I assumed that because he was well educated he would not be threatened by my professional status. I ignored cultural differences and the fact that his social drinking was frequently excessive.

I married within a year of being divorced and began to discover that my second husband was indeed in the same profession but had not learned anything new in ten years. I also quickly learned that our relationship began to totter as soon as I began to advance and get professional recognition. Furthermore, what I had seen as social drinking was rapidly becoming a problem.

Another man with a weak ego and addictive behaviors! What was the matter with me? Why did I choose this kind of man? Did the fact that I had been raised by unhappily married parents, that my mother had often been suicidal when I was a young child, and was still difficult now that I was grown, have anything to do with my present problems? What could I do to make things right? One divorce I could rationalize with the idea that everyone makes mistakes, particularly when they are young, but two divorces definitely placed responsibility on me. With this inner dialogue and much outer stress, I began therapy!

I had been in therapy before my first divorce. It was helpful. There was little confrontation and a great deal of quiet support. My therapist was intelligent, kind, and generally non-directive. Without the therapeutic support, I probably would not have had the confidence to get a divorce. At that time, and in the subculture to which I belonged, it was definitely not socially approved.

During the time of the legal proceedings, while I was dating, and before my second marriage, I pushed my problems aside by achieving professionally and keeping busy. After the second marriage began to become problematic, I managed by talking to friends, by continuing to work very hard, occasionally drinking a bit too much and smoking a great deal.

My husband and I were in conjoint therapy for a little while until I decided that the marriage had been a mistake. I began divorce proceedings and group therapy. I was extremely frightened and unknowingly curled up in what was almost a classical fetal position at the first group meeting.

The most valuable thing I learned was that I was lovable just for being me. I did not have to rescue others to justify my existence, get sick to get positive strokes, or constantly achieve in order to get affection.

Other valuable things that I learned included finding out about the importance of strokes and how to avoid getting stroke-deprived. The Karpman Triangle (see page 137) was a valuable guideline for me to remind myself to stop rescuing. I quickly absorbed the fact that most of the time that I felt "rotten" in relationships was when I was a rescuer.

I learned about gentle but effective confrontation, about treatment contracts, games, passivity, day-long workshops and treatment days, script decisions and redecisions. I also learned the importance of not discounting either the seriousness of a problem or my ability to solve it. In essence I learned to love and care for myself and to stop beating myself up. I learned to think differently about myself and therefore about others.

I expected a long-term treatment program and was surprised when after approximately six months my therapist tactfully suggested that since I had achieved my treatment goals I was ready to leave, unless I was aware of wanting anything else.

The first part of my treatment focused upon my getting affirmed, stroked, nurtured, and cared about for "being." Previously I had been deprived of recognition except for achievements. Next there were explanations and gentle confrontations of games, discounting, and passivity. I well recall my astonishment at discovering how passive I was. I was also encouraged to mourn my losses—real and fantasized. The last stages included script analysis and redecisions about living, belonging, and feeling. The final phase was a consolidation of gains.

I changed my life in many ways. I became much healthier physically. Colds, bronchitis, flu, etc., are no longer a part of my life, but rather a very rare occurrence.

I started to treat myself more kindly and less critically and therefore become friendlier and less judgmental with others. I dealt with my children more constructively and in general became both gentler and more assertive. I gave and received more strokes and so my life became warmer and richer. I enjoyed male companionship, but did not feel that I had to have a significant male in my life to be happy. I gained a whole new appreciation of the value of women friends. I advanced professionally because of increased skills and more self-confidence. I was less interested in always pleasing others and therefore became more creative.

I lived fully and years later met, fell in love with, and married an intelligent, sensitive, and loving man with whom I appreciatively share my life. I began to live with more joy than self-pity and more serenity than fear.

As a child, Jean had learned most of her lessons well. She was bright and highly motivated and a devoted mother. Her problem was that she had also been taught that she was a princess and was supposed to find a prince who'd look after her forever. She found two princes, but discovered when it was too late that they were both little boys looking for a good mommy who'd take care of them. When they did not get what they wanted, they became adolescents and decided they'd do as they pleased whether she liked it or not.

In therapy Jean discovered that although she was sophisticated and knowledgeable she had many unmet needs. Her own Child was sometimes very little and needy. As these needs were met Jean came to realize she no longer needed or wanted another prince. She discovered how good she felt when she had learned to take good care of herself, how to enjoy friends, and how to choose a mature man for mutual love, respect, and caring.

MAGGIE

Maggie was actually shaking when she came to her first therapy session. She was experiencing a panic attack because she honestly believed that she could not live without a man. Her husband had simply "walked out" of their home and wanted to end the marriage. Maggie was left with four children, one only a few months old, and she was scared.

However her therapy would move forward, right now something had to happen to stop her shaking. It was no time for talking. I began to show Maggie a deep relaxation response. I taught her how to breathe so that the tension in her muscles gradually eased and oxygen filled her body and the shaking stopped. When a person panics, as in Maggie's case, one of the observable signs is shortened breath, sometimes short gasps. At this lessening of oxygen, the person may then go into hyperventilation or be unable to get breath at all, which produces more panic. It took only a few moments for Maggie to begin to breathe rhythmically and deeply. Her body became quiet. Now we could talk.

Here is Maggie's account of her experiences in therapy.

Maggie's Story

My first experience with therapy grew out of my attending a series of sessions at my church on "managing stress." That's what I needed to learn to do; I was overwhelmed by the stress in my life at that time and was leaning heavily on my church and faith for support. Our priest recommended a therapist who by listening to and acknowledging the validity of my pain won my trust from the first day. Since then my continuing growth has not been painless, but the rewards of awareness and pride in myself have encouraged me to keep on.

I began therapy aware of a tremendous anger which at first I experienced as a feeling of fear. My husband had left me and our four children, one of whom was an infant. Verbally, Jim had said he wanted to be with us "next week," "next month," etc., but his actions never matched his words and promises, and he wasn't fulfilling his obligations as husband or father. I couldn't bring myself to believe that he was lying or that he really was walking out, so I kept hiding the truth from myself. My upbringing and my Catholic faith would not release me from my faith in my marriage even though I was neglecting myself and causing myself great pain. My self-esteem was at rock bottom. I was embarrassed and ashamed and hiding from everyone, even from myself. I was frightened at being a single parent but I hung on to a frayed thread of self-worth feelings. I seemed to have nothing else at the time.

Before I decided to begin therapy, endurance seemed the only answer to my problems, but I had become less and less confident as time went on and finally I was utterly exhausted trying to hang on.

In my therapy sessions I learned to distinguish reality from childish fantasy and I learned to think and to act rather than simply react to other people. I had spent most of my life doing what I thought people wanted me to do instead of thinking for myself and taking responsibility for myself, my decisions, and my actions.

It was very difficult for me to accept the situation I found myself in when my husband "walked out." When I was willing to be honest about what had happened, I saw that my life had taken a direction that was not of my desire or choosing but this was not a reflection on my character or my personality. I began to discover myself as an individual and not just see myself as wife or mother. I had ups and downs and I resisted many times, but I did begin to enjoy the new me. I learned that this slow process is normal and healthy; that was encouraging in itself. Self-acceptance had followed circumstance acceptance. I had lived so long with the "old" person! The new joy seemed too much to hope for, but it wasn't. It lasted.

I now own my negative feelings rather than believe that other people have caused them. And I own my positive ones too. My relationships with other people are now more manageable and more fun. Today, when I feel stress, I recapture the comfort and security that is mine through realizing my self-worth, being in touch with my feelings, and knowing how to relate to other people.

I have grown to like myself and to appreciate myself. My family and friends seem to appreciate all that I have learned through therapy. My children especially have gained by witnessing my life experiences guided by my good counselors. I think I am a much better parent than I was and so do my children.

It is too bad that good regular therapy is not an automatic occurrence in everyone's life rather than a frantic grasp for help in crisis or desperation. I am very grateful to God for my therapy.

Maggie was raised in the South in a family of proud history and tradition. The Old Southern gentility and feminine modeling had imprinted themselves well on Maggie. She had left college without a degree to marry her "gallant major." She had been a perfect wife, mother, and Catholic. Her dress was beautiful, her manners charming, her sweetness genuine. The problem was that she was "Maggie of the mirror." She reflected her historically fine and proud family, her firmly-established religion, her genteel community. Pleasant as all this was, Maggie had never known who she was. She was angry because intuitively she knew she had never found herself, and she was afraid because she thought she lacked the courage to "break free."

Our first job was to look at the fear. What was Maggie's catastrophic fear? What would happen if she didn't have a man and if she then began to find herself? When Maggie finally saw that it was her three-year-old inner Child who believed she could not survive alone, she decided to take care of that little inner Child and not let her determine her life. This done, Maggie was ready to live in the Now. The first task was a practical one. How could she support her children financially and plan for the future? When, sometime later, two of her children went off to college on scholarships and work-study programs, Maggie decided to finish her own college degree by taking night courses.

The last step came when Maggie decided that she was no longer willing to live with her husband's lies and irresponsibility. He had kept returning home for short visits and Maggie had kept hoping they could work things out. Finally she knew she didn't want him to return. It was difficult for her to go against her family's and her church's teaching, but Maggie now knew who she was and what she was choosing. The shaking Maggie who had entered therapy was now the Maggie who had become her own woman. Someday she would like to marry again, this time not out of fear and lack of self-worth, but out of joy.

Low Self-Esteem

ANN

When Ann first came to my office several years ago, I had the image of two Anns walking down a long path. One looked down, and it was as though she had all she could do to drag herself along to keep up with the other. The other looked energetic and friendly, greeted all who passed with words and a smile, and looked just fine. While each Ann was aware that the other was there and stayed parallel, they did not look at, touch, or show any recognition of the other.

Outwardly Ann appeared to be confident and composed. She expressed her thoughts with clarity and precision. Almost objectively and without emotion, she told of her fear that she was about to lose her mind and of the anguish in her life. Her facade, which was beginning to crumble, was concealing a huge amount of fear, anger, and sadness. Not only was Ann keeping secrets from her family and friends, she was keeping them from herself. She had never allowed herself to know the depth or nature of her pain. She was aware of the facts and of what she thought, but her feelings were all but dead.

As a therapist, I work with the assumption that once things are brought into the open they are not nearly as frightening as when they are kept hidden, avoided, or denied. It is only when they are in the open that they can be evaluated, put to rest, or acted upon in a conscious way. My first task with Ann was for the two of us to begin to gain an understanding of the nature of her fears. I assured her that she could get to know herself at her own pace and in such a way that she could become her own best friend.

I recommended that Ann come into group therapy, with the options of individual sessions on request. I favored group as her primary therapy mode because I knew that in group she would gain acceptance, encouragement, and support from the group members as well as from me. Also, she would have the opportunity to observe others venturing into the frightening and dark places within themselves and coming out not only unscathed, but victorious.

Ann's Story

I thought I was on the verge of losing my mind. I had been in a marriage for ten years with someone I didn't want to be married to, and didn't care for. I was so out of touch with my feelings that I couldn't look in the mirror and know who I was any more. I constantly thought about divorce, but had many reasons why I shouldn't get divorced, all based on other people's perceptions of my husband, and my own perception that there must be something wrong with me. If everyone else thought he was so wonderful, why couldn't I? There must be a problem with me since I couldn't love him the way he deserved to be loved.

Two things happened that sent me to the telephone to find someone to talk to about my life. The first was that my daughter, who was seven, came home from school one day, walked into the kitchen, looked up at me with tears in her eyes, and said, "Mommy, why don't you smile any more?" That burst my illusion that I was still functioning and that the children were unaware of my pain. It also threatened my resolve to stay married and shield my children from the pain which I knew divorce could bring them. I realized I'd been so emotionally distant from the children that I had scarcely related to them at all in over a year.

The second thing that happened was that I went into the bathroom one morning after the children had gone to school. When I looked in the mirror I literally couldn't relate to the face.

I was so out of touch with myself that it was like looking at a stranger. That was a very frightening feeling. It was similar to what I think an "out of body" experience must be like. I knew then that I had gone beyond the point where I was able to handle things alone. I needed someone to talk to. I was completely disassociated from my feelings. I spent all my time focusing on "what if's." What if I divorce my husband? What would he feel? What would happen to the children? I never bothered to ask myself what I was thinking or feeling. I realized I didn't love my husband and the marriage was nothing but a facade, but I couldn't bring myself to tell anyone. I knew I needed therapy.

I had tried a number of things. I surrounded myself with friends and nice people. I see now, in looking back, the best way I was able to distance myself from my husband was to see to it that the house was full of friends and family. I was able to stay involved with them and not with him. I tried to solve the problem with alcohol. Using alcohol was the only way in which I could have any kind of physical relationship with him at all.

I had gone into therapy with a psychiatrist fairly soon after we were married. I had problems even then with having any kind of sexual relationship, and my husband pronounced that I must be frigid. I bought that and went into therapy. Psychiatry was not helpful. The psychiatrist put me on Valium. I didn't stay on it very long because I didn't feel it was helping the problem at all. Then, less than a year after I was married, I launched into an affair. It was a torrid affair, which didn't help the problem with my husband, but I knew I wasn't frigid! I think I was so trapped that I just felt like I wasn't alive. I was also just twenty years old and was not using very good judgment. I had married on the rebound from a traumatic love affair, followed by an acquaintance rape. I married out of fear, not out of any kind of good feelings.

Endurance characterizes what I tried for years. I put on a "happy face" and I lived a life of my own that was a secret life. I lived in my head. I was constantly thinking and plotting about what my life would be like if I weren't in the relationship with my husband. I constantly strategized about how I would handle the divorce if I were to get it, but I never had the courage to look him in the eye and say, "It's over, I want out." About six months before I came into therapy I told my husband about my unhappiness and he suggested we go to see the priest at the Episcopal church we were then attending. But I was told by the priest that I talked too much, that I was frightening my husband by being so verbal, and that I should learn to express my opinions less. I knew from that response that the priest was not going to be any source of help to me, and I refused to go back. The next step was to find a therapist and I was referred to you.

The first thing that was different was that you offered both group and one-to-one therapy. I started out in group. I had never been in a group before; I had never shared my feelings, or had any kind of acknowledgment that my feelings were valid. Always, in psychiatry, I felt like it was just me and the psychiatrist. He was sitting in judgment, and I didn't get any kind of feedback; I didn't get much reinforcement either. Coming into group and hearing other people, being able to know that I was not alone, that my feelings were valid, that it was all right to feel the way I felt, was very reinforcing. It was the first time that I had ever been able to admit that I didn't love my husband, and that I needed to start living life honestly. Group was very helpful. When I had some individual sessions I was able to trust enough to do some "little work" (see Part Two). I was able to go back and look at some things that had been very frightening to me before and I felt safe in a way that I had not known previously. I felt safe enough to look at my mother, to be a little kid again, and to question my adoring relationship with my father. I discovered I could let somebody know who I was and what I was thinking and feeling and still be accepted.

The most valuable thing I learned was that it is all right to feel what I feel, to say what I think, and it is all right for me to be different from other people.

Another valuable thing I learned is that I am not responsible for all the feelings of all the other people I care about in the world.

As I grew up, I had absorbed the notion that if other people had bad feelings, somehow it was my duty to take care of those people, protect them, and make them happy. Learning that I was responsible for what I think, how I feel, and how I act and that I am not responsible for what other people think, feel, and do was a very liberating and valuable thing for me. At the same time it has also been the hardest thing to learn.

I characterize the first stage in my therapy as being the time when I learned that I could trust other people to hear me and not be judgmental about what they were hearing. That came about in the very early stages of group.

The second stage was the stage of anger. I was angry and had a lot of bad feelings about what I had been doing to myself. I felt as if I had betrayed myself. While I was learning a lot I was unforgiving of what I thought I had done to myself. I think that deep down inside I felt as though I deserved to be punished in some way for something. I went through a stage where I basically punished myself with agonizing regrets.

The next stage was what I characterize as a long exploration. It was like a voyage, not down a long straight river, but through a jungle river, going up and down little tributaries. Each tributary was a painful part of my life, either a painful experience or a painful relationship or an exploration of things about myself that I didn't have any conscious understanding of before.

First, there were my mother's addiction to drugs and her depression. Then there was the fear that I was going to "lose my mind" because my mother and my grandfather had both spent times with nervous breakdowns in mental institutions. And there was the fear that if I ever let my feelings out I would never be able to control them. I had controlled them for so long! By now I had a fantasy that if I ever started to cry I would never be able to stop. There was also the realization that my father had deserted me when I was a child by requiring that I shut off my feelings. He had told me that I couldn't express my feelings to him or my mother because we had to protect her by keeping up a facade of happiness, of everything being well at home.

Through this long exploration I began to understand how I behaved after I began these journeys. I had always had a sense of what I was like inside, but I hadn't ever known why I was like that. Suddenly, all of this knowledge was beginning to be available to me. While it was on the one hand often very painful, on the other hand it gave me an enormous sense of relief to know that none of this was anything that I couldn't deal with and handle. That was really the prelude to the fourth stage, understanding that nothing about me that I didn't want to have did I have to keep; that I was not destined to be my mother or to behave like my mother, or to have a fate that I couldn't control, or to respond in ways that I couldn't control. Coming to that realization was extremely important, and it empowered me in a way that I had never been empowered before.

It was okay to come back to therapy occasionally to check things out. I still feel that way and I am comfortable knowing that therapy is always available for me to deal with things that I don't feel safe or comfortable with all by myself.

I've changed my life in the sense that I don't have as many fears. I know that I am not going to end up being just like my mother. I know that I am a different person. I have developed an appreciation for myself and for the kind of person that I am.

There are still problems that I work on, particularly the ownership of other people's feelings. But, a change that's positive and one that I think about a lot is the fact that I recognize when I am doing that. Now when I know that is happening, I can say, "Wait a minute. Is that the way I want to deal with this, or do I want to do something different?" That's been a big change. I act out of consciousness. I can think. In some areas, I will probably always first have an emotional "kick." I will not feel what I want to feel. But I do know now that when I get those bad feelings I can think and get past them. I'm comfortable with that, and that's a change that was necessary and a change that I welcome.

As a small child Ann decided, "Unless I take care of everyone and make them happy a terrible tragedy will happen—someone will go crazy and it will be my fault." Along with this decision she developed the following belief system: Other people's needs are more important than mine. I'm responsible for how other people feel. If I do just the right thing everyone will be happy.

What Ann did not realize was that she had no power to make anyone else feel happy. She was living with a set of magical childhood conclusions based on false assumptions. She was unaware of her own needs and preoccupied with her inability to control her husband's feelings. She had concluded that she was bad. She felt so helpless and hopeless that she feared continuing the family pattern of "going crazy."

In our initial interview I explored with Ann her fears about going crazy, how she would do that, and what purpose it would serve. She knew the answers immediately, and was visibly relieved once her fears were out in the open. She made a contract with herself that she would find constructive ways of solving problems without going crazy.

In the months that followed Ann became an active participant in group therapy. Initially she freely expressed her needs in relationship to her family, but was at a loss when someone asked her about herself as an individual. She had trouble believing that anyone was interested in how she felt or what she wanted for herself. She was always in the forefront when group members asked for support or nurturing. The only time I ever saw her stuck for words was when she was asked what she'd like to receive from others.

Gradually Ann trusted the group and herself enough to allow herself to know and to say how she felt. The first time she did this and found that no one criticized and no one left her she was amazed. She looked about three years old. Scared at first, but when she realized nothing terrible had happened, radiant with joy.

Soon after that she had the courage to relive many of her traumatic childhood experiences and make new decisions about herself and her world. Ann began a whole new learning experience. She came to know she is entitled to have wants and needs and that her needs can be met without harming other people. Ann learned that she is all right no matter what she feels, and she can express her feelings without hurting herself or others. She also came to know that she is good and she does not need to be perfect.

As she grew to become her own best friend, Ann found that she was becoming a better friend to others.

JOHANNA

Something about Johanna caught my attention. I was speaking to a group of people who had come to find out what therapy was all about. Johanna sat directly in front of me and listened to every word. She was in her early twenties and obviously eager for learning and life. A few minutes' informal conversation at the coffee hour let me know that here was a vibrant, exciting person with a keen mind. She decided to come to a weekend conference I was giving and then told me that she wanted to train to become a psychotherapist. That training involved three things: 1) mastering information, 2) individual therapy to get her psychological house in order, and 3) evidencing competency in clinical skills.

At the end of the conference, Johanna knew what would be involved in her training. For her, "this was it." The decision was to change her career from college teaching to psychotherapy and start her on an eight-year course.

Johanna's Story

Perhaps the most clearly identified problems I had were marital. But longer standing were my underlying depression and my low self-esteem! I had had many problems with my mother and with my feminine identity. I tended to deny my sexuality, my anger, and my worth as a person.

I had read a great deal in the popular press and had been in encounter groups and support groups. My husband and I had participated in a couples' enrichment group, had tried talking things out with each other, had had drug experiences (marijuana and LSD), and had practiced open marriage.

When I came into therapy, I began to focus on specific issues that were dragging me down and causing me pain. I began to learn about taking responsibility for myself and to center in on my own process. I realized that I could change myself. This involved two things: 1) I needed to trust myself and my own process of change; 2) I needed to trust that my problems could be resolved by thinking through and exploring my feelings.

When I think back to my early twenties, what stands out to me is my naiveté and innocence—well-guarded systems of denial which I had developed to protect me from the pain and anger of my childhood. I had learned to shield myself from my mother's narcissism and depression, had felt guilty for my parents' marital problems, and had avoided my own feelings by literally numbing myself with work and activity.

As a young adult I had found it difficult to find a direction for myself because I was so out of touch with my own thoughts and feelings. It was as if I were asleep, yet functioning externally.

In therapy I learned to pay attention to myself. I learned that I could identify my feelings and know that my feelings were guideposts to my internal motivation. I also learned that I could think about what I felt and believed and could sort out irrational belief systems in myself and others.

My first awakening happened in an encounter group when another group member confronted me about not liking myself. He was right and my "cover" of sweetness was blown off. From encounter groups and my reading in the popular press, I learned that there were options to other ways of thinking and acting.

T.A. training and therapy put the focus for change back on myself. I learned to articulate my feelings, thoughts, beliefs, and wants. I experimented with "social control," willing myself to be different. My self-concept began to change as a result of what I told myself about myself as well as from the strokes and support I received from the group members and my therapist. This new sense of competence and worth was an important foundation for additional work.

Through redecision work, reparenting/regressive work, I began the process of sorting out early influences. I began to deal with old ghosts which were haunting me (my mother's narcissism, my father's passivity) and to realize how those had affected my childhood and later life. I also began to appreciate my parents' strengths (my mother's creativity and initiative, and my father's nurturing and support).

I made a number of changes in my life as a result of all the encounter groups, reading, and therapy. I discovered my husband and spent time learning about myself. I improved my self-concept, I became more assertive, more emotionally expressive, and more trusting of my feelings. As I understood the dynamics of my early life, I became more free of my early decisions. I stopped rebelling against my mother and allowed myself to embrace my own kind of femininity and to express this. I left my teaching post and changed my career.

Today, Dr. Johanna is the same special, vibrant, exciting person she was when first we met. She is still eager for learning and life. She is an excellent psychotherapist and is also teaching in a college. When I see her now, I remember the twenty-five-year old girl sitting in front of me and I admire the forty-year-old woman who worked so honestly and courageously to become herself.

Isolation

SARA

For several years I conducted a section of the training programs provided for telephone crisis line volunteer workers. My assignment was to teach volunteers how to handle calls from people who were depressed or suicidal. Shortly after one of these events, Maree, the counselor who had organized the program, called to tell me she had referred Sara to me and asked if I would be willing to work with her. Maree described Sara as chronically depressed, frequently suicidal, and most recently having had several catatonic episodes when she stared into space and did not move or talk for hours at a time. She had been hospitalized frequently. She did not want another hospitalization and had indicated that she was willing to come to see me.

I had worked with many suicidal people but no one who had been catatonic. I was willing to see her for an evaluation to assess whether we would be likely to work well together. Normally, I require that people call me to make their own appointments. However, since Sara was catatonic at the time and therefore not talking, I decided to write her a letter. I was willing to see her only on condition that she stop all suicide attempts, gestures, or threats.

In the letter I explained that as long as she operated on the conviction that if things got bad enough she could kill herself she was likely to allow that to happen. However, as soon as she decided that no matter what happened she'd find a way to deal with the situation, she'd no longer keep on allowing her situation to get out of hand.

There were two reasons for my being willing to see her on that condition. One was that until she gave up the option of suicide she would not have the motivation to solve her problems. Second, if she was going to kill herself anyway, coming to see me would be a waste of her time, energy, and money. I was also convinced that if she had been 100 percent suicidal she would have made sure one of her many attempts had worked.

I did not expect that she would immediately make a lifelong decision not to commit suicide, since she did not know me and had no reason to trust that I would stick with her and support her during her healing process. I did expect that each time she came she would make a commitment to keep her next appointment until she made a permanent decision.

Initially I arranged to see her for two individual appointments weekly, each for half an hour.

Sara's Story

I had been seeing a counselor from a crisis center for several months. I had been severely depressed, with suicidal thoughts. It had become harder and harder to function—to get out of bed—to work—to accomplish anything. I was becoming more and more withdrawn and feeling more and more hopeless.

The counselor I had been seeing told me she knew a psychotherapist and asked me if I would be willing to see her. I was very hesitant. I thought I just could not go over all the things that had happened in my life again with someone else. My life was not worth it anyway. Second, I had not been able to change anything, it was always going to be the same, so why go? I told her I would think about it. She asked me if I would give her permission to talk to this person about me and why she wanted to refer me to her.

I did think about going to see her and had just decided I would not do it when I got a letter from her. She said she thought she could help me and that I was worth it. I cried when I read the letter. I did not think that anyone could actually care about me. Then I wondered why she even wanted to help me. I felt sure that if she got to know what a terrible person I was she would change her mind.

Having made a contract with the crisis counselor, I made and kept an appointment with her. The date happened to be my birthday. I think now how fitting that was, for it was the beginning of a whole new way of living. It was a "rebirth."

Up to this time in my life I had been chronically depressed. Now my sadness and hopelessness about my life were overwhelming, and I could see no end to my misery. As I recall the first several sessions I had with her, I was unable to express myself verbally. Yet I thought I would never stop crying. She often asked me what I wanted or what I needed and I had absolutely no idea. I had no concept of "want" or "need." I had never mattered to anyone else. Most of my life had been spent in taking care of someone else's needs or wants, and my times of feeling best about myself came when I was doing things for other people. Then they were happy and I thought they liked me. But I could never give enough or do enough or be good enough. I was never enough. I had little or no self-esteem and had spent all my life wanting to be somebody else.

I was living my life with many rules to guide me. I had never made a decision on my own, even as an adult, because I was never allowed or taught to make decisions as a child. I felt I had no control over my life.

From the age of twelve onward I spent many hours in different therapies. I saw mostly psychiatrists because that is what my insurance covered. For years I was on medications including Thorazine, Melliril, and Stelazine. I remember that sometimes during these periods I felt nothing.

When I was twelve, the psychiatrist I saw convinced me that he cared about me and that it would be a good experience for me to learn to be close to him sexually. After months of this it just did not feel right and I started not to trust him. I told him I did not want to see him any more. He told me that if I told my parents he would tell them that I was lying or crazy and he would commit me to a mental hospital. (My parents would have believed him because I used to lie often and that was one of the reasons I was seeing him in the first place.) I continued to see him for about six months, until we moved to another city.

Following that I had several hospitalizations for depression and attempted suicides. Several of these stays in hospitals lasted for three to four months. When I was nineteen or twenty I had a series of shock treatments. Before I started psychotherapy I had made some attempt at suicide every spring for years. I managed to get through the winters knowing spring would come. Spring came, the world became bright and new again, yet I remained the same inside. My life became no better and I felt more hopeless.

In therapy for the first time in my life I felt someone else really cared how I felt and what happened to me. Subsequently, I realized that I am worth caring about.

Overall, I don't think I was helped by the other therapies. I was very afraid of life—I know now I was always in a victim position—and I was even more afraid of my thoughts. I was out of touch with any feeling other than sadness. I felt I had no control over my own life and believed that other people were more important than I was. I believed that other people were responsible for how I reacted and for everything that happened to me. I had no sense of being responsible for myself and no idea of what life meant. I had no conception that being in charge of my own life was even possible, let alone how I could do it.

No other therapist ever confronted me with the fact that I could change what I was doing, that I could stop my destructive behavior, and that being responsible could be wonderful and exciting. The psychiatrists I had seen did no more than listen to me talk and I did not tell them much about me because I thought my thoughts made me such a terrible person. Each and every one of them put me on medication. Nothing was ever said to me about this or that seeming to be a problem for me. I was never asked such things as how could I change what I was doing to help myself feel better or what was I willing to do toward solving a problem.

Looking back at it now, I don't even consider that I was ever in therapy before. There was no action. The psychiatrists were all passive. I was passive. They were willing—and silently encouraging me—to stay in the same place. At the time I did not question that. I believed that is what it was supposed to be and that as long as I took my medication I was doing what I was supposed to do. Yet, I never felt OK. It was like a game I played with myself and everyone I knew. I knew how to appear "normal" even if I knew I wasn't.

The most important thing I learned from this therapy is that I am a wonderful human being just the way I am. I had so much to learn that it became a complete reeducation for me. Learning that I have choices and am responsible for what I say, what I feel, and what I do was an amazing revelation. Discovering that I had those choices and that I was good felt so good. I learned to love myself and trust myself, and that led to learning to love and trust others. Previously I had no idea of what loving was about. All I did was try to please others, and I felt awful when that did not work.

I learned that I can say "no" without guilt and that others will not die when I don't do what they want. I also discovered that I can identify what I need and what I want and that sometimes needs and wants are not at all the same. Learning that I can take care of myself feels like a miracle. I had never entertained the possibility before. I know now that not only can I ask, I can also accept whatever the other person's response may be. As it turns out, the response is almost always positive.

Previously I had always believed I had to guess what other people wanted. I learned how to ask them directly. It is much easier that way! All of these things have enabled me to be able to communicate openly and honestly.

I discovered that much of my depression was the result of my not being in touch with how much anger I had inside of me and how to deal with that. As a child I was allowed to be depressed and sad, but not to be angry. During therapy I learned how to stay in the here and now and to be in touch with how I was feeling as events occur.

I started out feeling sad, depressed, hopeless, and helpless. I did not talk about this at all at first. All I was able to do was to sit and cry or fight back tears. I felt terrible and yet was not able to open my mouth. My head was full of horrible events of the past. I had written reams and reams about some of my memories, and one day took a few pages into my session for my therapist to read. Even when she made comments or asked questions about what I had written, I did not know how to answer. I did know that she was interested and she actually asked me to bring in more any time I wanted.

When I was still not speaking, she told me that I looked very scared and very little. She also said she thought the roots of my problems went back to when I was very little and that I had not learned that it was good that I was alive or that I was loved and wanted. My therapist told me that when people's needs are not met when they are little that has an effect on them throughout their lives, but it doesn't mean they have to be deprived forever. She told me about reparenting and that she was willing to do some reparenting with me during my sessions. She would start out by holding me as if I were a few months old.

Being held felt good from the start, but soon she told me if I wanted to be held again I would have to ask. I could do that by crying or I could just ask. I hated having to ask. During this time I moved from feeling hopeless to realizing that maybe there would be a time when I would feel better. I started to feel less depressed than I had felt in many years. I knew someone cared what happened to me and I started to feel I was worth something.

Next I realized that I was the one who was going to have to do the work. No one else could make my life better for me. After I made a no-suicide contract, I knew I no longer had a way out and I was going to have to do something for myself. I could not and would not go on with my life the way it had been. After this so much happened and so quickly that I do not remember the order of my progression.

As I started to trust myself, I dealt with some past experiences that I had not allowed myself to feel angry about or deal with up to this point. Each time I thought of one of these experiences it was as fresh in my mind as if it had happened yesterday. I learned I could allow myself to feel angry, express my anger, and then let it go. Up until then my past had been with me all the time. I went on reliving and recalling horrible memories over and over again. Everywhere I went, every new experience I had, I still had those old memories. My mind was so full of those old events that I could not see any new experience as it was. Now, I can remember when I choose to do so, but I do it with an emotional distance so that the memories do not interfere with my life as it is here and now.

As a result of therapy, my life is quite different and very good. Each day brings with it many new challenges, more fun experiences, more self-knowledge, more sharing, more of the excitement of living a full life. And it is all real! Even the "hard stuff" is easier now because I have built into my brain a whole new system for processing what is happening and what I want to happen. How I think and feel about myself is 180° away from where I was before I met you. You believed in me enough to teach me to believe in myself.

Another change was to open up honestly to other people. I'm more trusting and less judgmental of myself and others, and I am much more flexible than I ever believed possible. I think about options much more than "shoulds." I no longer worry the way I did; I can see plainly now that it was a totally non-productive activity for me. I take more risks—I am much less scared, and I have much more fun!

What I wish for so many people is that they too will learn to love themselves. How can we truly love others until we can do that? For me it has been the answer to living a fuller and much happier life. I feel as if I have been given a "new start." It is not that my previous life has been erased but that it has shifted to the side, where it stays for the good memories. Before, I would have questioned how that could happen. I don't question now. It just is.

When Sara first came she hardly said a word. For several weeks she came with pages of things she had written for me to read. Initially she wrote about her suicide attempts and how she felt about herself. Then she began to write about some of the traumatic experiences she had had.

She told how her father had always emphasized how important it was that she walk to school on the sidewalks. Under no circumstances was she to take the shortcut through the woods. She did walk to school on the sidewalks, but she took the shortcut home! One day when she was eight or nine a man met her in the woods and raped her. She was so fearful that her father would punish her if he ever found out she had ventured through the woods alone that she told no one about the rape. For years she carried the burden of that secret alone. The memory still haunted her. Every time she thought of it she convinced herself more deeply that she was evil and bad beyond belief.

Another horrible memory was having been in an automobile accident. She was the driver and her passenger, her best friend at the time, was killed. Even though someone else was considered responsible for the accident, she felt that she had been responsible for her friend's death and was even more certain that she was a thoroughly bad and unlovable person.

In her story, Sara wrote about being unable to talk, or ever stop crying. In reality, all of her crying was kept inside. I never saw a tear. Her eyes were clear. Sometimes she looked at me and sometimes into space. She sat perfectly still but her mouth moved constantly. Sometimes it looked as if she was trying to say something with her lips pressed closed. At other times it looked more as though she was making sucking movements.

After a few sessions I knew from her writing that she felt hopeless, abandoned, unworthy of living, and unlovable. I told her about "Little Work" and said I would be willing to do some reparenting with her for part of each session. However, she would need to ask to be held. She could either cry or ask verbally. After much struggling she did ask and she loved it. She continued to make hard work of it and seldom asked until the last few minutes of her sessions. One day she refused to ask. When I told her it was time to go, she stood up, stamped her foot, and shouted, "I hate you," and stomped out of the room. I was delighted; I knew she was well on her way!

After that she always asked early, and she began to talk and made strides in her healing process. Not only did she have a symbolic rebirth, but she grew to be a beautiful, confident, and productive woman who radiates warmth.

After the Mental Hospital

KRYS

A psychiatrist who was leaving town referred the twelve people who were in her two therapy groups to me. I visited the groups for their last two sessions with her. Krys was one of the members.

From the start Krys was the clown of the group. Each week she came with humorous anecdotes and comical behavior. However, she seldom related directly to the other members, and often withdrew.

At the first meeting with me, Krys was the life of the party until the group gathered for its work. Initially she sat and stared—sometimes into space, sometimes at another group member, sometimes at me. Then gradually she focused more and more on me. She said nothing but her big brown eyes, very young face, and short, fast, deep breaths seemed to be saying, "Please, please, please!"

Krys's Story

When I first came to see this therapist, I was depressed and tired of my life as it was and had been for years. I was existing and not living. I wanted to be nursed, nurtured, and held, but I had no one I could touch or who touched me. I was having auditory hallucinations, primarily related to self-mutilation. As far as I could, I was blocking out all of my emotional and physical feelings.

I was extremely suicidal. Sometimes I thought of this on a conscious level, and at other times the ideas came through my hallucinations. At times I looked forward to my hallucinations, because it was then that I felt in control. I would "flirt with death," so to speak. For example, I was working second shift and had a fifty-mile drive home. On the highway I'd periodically get up to the speed limit and then close my eyes to test how long I could keep them closed. Since I had no intention of harming anyone else I'd open my eyes to make sure no one was in danger. Also, I hoarded pills. Sometimes I was scared, knowing that I had enough to kill myself, and at other times it was a comfort to know I was in control over my life or death.

Before my therapy I often fantasized about death. I'd sit for hours at the lake and think about just slipping into the water and swimming toward the other side until I couldn't swim any further. (The only time I actually attempted suicide I slit my wrists and took pills.)

I was not happy at home. I had to endure feelings of isolation and lack of concern. The rule there was that you didn't talk unless you had something important to say, and I was generally told to be quiet because I wasn't saying something important—at least my parents didn't think it was important. So I began living in a world of my own within my head, hearing voices and slowly losing all sense of feelings, both physical and emotional. The voices often told me to cut myself. When I did that, it gave me reassurance that I was alive. When I saw blood run down my arm or leg, this meant life.

I built a wall around me. I practiced at not feeling. For years, I would not let myself cry. I'd laugh at things but I had to force myself to do that. I did not want other people to think there was something wrong with me.

I'd been in therapy with several different doctors. Most of the psychiatrists were helpful only in the beginning of therapy. One of the issues I needed to deal was with incest and molestation by my grandfather. Over and over their resolution to the problem seemed to be my having a positive sexual experience with them. At that point I would terminate therapy and feel more strongly that there was something wrong with me. Then I sought counseling from my minister. He, in turn, attempted to have a sexual relationship with me. I quit church altogether for a long period of time. I felt like a terrible person.

I started taking medications. I took enough to keep me sedated to the point of not having to feel but not enough that I could not function. Soon I quit seeing anyone professionally and discovered alcohol. I had had some experience with alcohol as a teenager. Adult drinking was serious. I drank to the point of not having to feel or to think. I just felt numb.

I had several forced hospitalizations. The first was at a university hospital, where I had what was called hysterical blindness. I lost my sight for three weeks. After three months I was given sodium pentathol and transported to a state hospital without my knowledge. While there I was restrained and "controlled" with Thorazine and Stelazine. My parents signed me out and took me home for a week, but I deteriorated and had terrible headaches. Then my mother took me to the local hospital and had me admitted to the psychiatric ward, where I stayed for a month.

The doctor told me to write my autobiography, and I spent a great of time writing about everything, including my grandfather, the minister, and my home life. When I gave it to the doctor he looked at it for about five seconds and ripped it up in front of me, saying that I hadn't told him anything. At that point I tried to break out. For days I begged to see the doctor. I sat in the hall outside the nursing station for hours each day only to discover he was leaving by the back door. My parents would not take me home, he would not see me, no one talked to me. I felt like I was "going nuts."

Finally, I became violent. I smashed a soft drink bottle and took a nurse hostage. I was afraid of hurting anybody and I cut myself instead. I felt like nobody and wanted to die. The very next day when I went into the hallway I found my suitcase packed with all of my things. "Hooray," I thought, "I'm getting out." I was, but once again, I was being sent to the state hospital, indefinitely and without ever seeing a judge.

Then I began to have hallucinations. I learned not to talk and so began to have conversations in my head. I did not get into any

trouble with people that way, and I could say everything I wanted to say. After megadoses of Thorazine and several rounds of
ECT (shock treatments) the doctor there ordered tests for my
headaches and found I had encephalitis. Finally, someone who
had some authority listened. Those awful headaches had not been
psychosomatic after all. With the right treatment and medication,
my headaches stopped.

I knew I had emotional problems that needed to be dealt with.
I began to talk to my doctor, who understood my plight and finally discharged me. I moved to another city and found a job. The
first psychiatrist I went to told me he was sexually attracted to me,
and so referred me to someone else. The referral doctor wanted to
be sexual with me. Each time this happened, I felt more and more
convinced that I was an evil person and was causing all of this.
Once again I retreated into conversations in my own head and decided to find a female psychiatrist. I did. She started me in group
therapy and later referred me to one of the authors.

The most important thing I learned in group therapy was that I
am lovable. Even though my parents said I wasn't, I am not just a
sex object. I am worthy in and of myself. I don't have to be perfect
in order to be loved. Love does not mean sex, as I was once led to
believe. Love is sharing, caring, and being at peace with accepting
that love. Before I started group therapy, I did not know what a
good friend was. Each time I started knowing someone, I felt
scared. I was not able to feel accepted or included. I now have ten
dear friends who do care about, love, and accept me as I am.

Therapy gave me a real sense of being. I learned to separate
what was fantasy from the "real world." My life became less frag-
mented. At first I seemed to have to analyze most of my thoughts
and conversations. Knowing whether my thoughts were coming
from my Parent, Adult, or Child helped me to understand much
about myself. When I realized that about 95 percent of my thoughts
were coming from my Critical Parent, I realized why I felt scared
so much of the time. Coming to understand this framework, I was
able to see how my life could and did change. I allowed myself to
be held and nurtured and so learned about unconditional love.

The first phase was learning to sort out my thoughts and where they came from. I learned how to stop the crazy thinking in my head. I also allowed myself to be touched and hugged by my therapist and the other members of my group. That was a big step. I could hug and be hugged and it was OK.

Next I began to allow myself to feel my feelings. This was hard. At the start of therapy I had been pretty much a zero with virtually no emotional or physical feelings. Transactional Analysis taught me it is OK for me to have feelings and needs, and it is all right to have my needs met. It wasn't threatening.

In the next phase I was ready for a re-parenting contract. My therapist already had contracts with two other people, and that was as many as she felt she could do at one time, so she referred me to two colleagues for re-parenting contracts. I had a new Mom and Dad. While being re-parented, I was allowed to regress to being under a year old, to be held, nurtured, bottle-fed, and stroked. This was the core of my beginning to know I am indeed lovable. As my needs were met, I gradually became an older child. I broke my reparenting contract with my contractual Mom when I became jealous when she also began to re-parent other people. However, I kept my contract with my new Dad, and as I grew up we became very good friends. We had a wonderful and healthy relationship.

Some time later I went back to my primary therapist to get lots more nurturing. This time I did not go back to her looking for a Mom but for a caring person to reaffirm my OKness. At this final stage of my therapy she also taught me to do self-hypnosis. This still helps me today. Therapy started my road to self-confidence and autonomy. I am now about to make plans and look forward to the future. I am living and not just existing. I am now more trusting and less suspicious and am able to form and keep close relationships. Life is still a challenge, and I accept this. I can look forward to fun, to reward, and to fulfillment. I am glad I survived, and I look forward to a bright future.

Krys was a challenge from the start. She came to the second group meeting I was leading with a three-inch scar on her arm where she had slashed herself during the week. She pulled up her

sleeve and revealed several scars from previous slashings—all
self-inflicted. She told how the voices in her head had told her she
had to do that. She explained that as long as she resisted, her tension increased and as soon as she slashed herself, she felt relief.
Our interaction proceeded something like this:

Therapist: What do the voices say?
Krys: You're bad, you deserve to be punished.
Therapist: What do you say to them?
Krys: Nothing, I just listen.
Therapist: What happens then?
Krys: I get more and more tense.
Therapist: And then...?
Krys: I feel so guilty...I get so tense I can't stand it any
            more and I slash myself. Then I feel better. Only
            then can I get any sleep.
Therapist: Whose voices are they?
Krys: I've never thought about it.
Therapist: Think about it now.
Krys: I'm too scared to do that. They'll kill me. (She
            stared into space.)
Therapist: Krys. Look at me. (She still stared into space.)
            (More firmly) Krys, look at me now. (She turned to
            me and her eyes looked like saucers.) That's not
            true. Voices cannot kill you.
Krys: But that's what they tell me.
Therapist: They may tell you that, but it's a lie. It is nothing
            but a big fat lie. Has anyone lied to you before?
Krys: Yes, often.
Therapist: You don't have to believe everything you hear.
            Voices can sound scary, but they cannot kill you.
Krys: (Looking and sounding about three years of age) I
            don't have to believe them?
Therapist: No, you don't. Look around the room, and ask two
            people here what they think about scaring yourself
            by believing lies. (She did that and got confirma-
            tion of what I had said.) Go and sit next to the per-

son you feel safest with in here. (She sat next to Judy and asked her to hold her hand.) Good, that's taking care of yourself. Now, I'll ask you again. Whose voices are they?

Krys: Are you sure they won't kill me?

Therapist: Yes. I'm sure.

Krys: My Mom and my Dad. (She immediately stared into space again. It took time to get her to look at me again.)

Therapist: Where are your Mom and Dad?

Krys: About 45 miles from here.

Therapist: You're absolutely sure they are not in your head?

Krys: Yes, but I can hear them now.

Therapist: Hearing voices in your head is the way you scare yourself. Your mother and father are miles away, but you carry their voices around in your head. They are not here. You are, and you are scaring yourself. Look at me and listen. I'm going to tell you something very important. Stop doing that! Scaring yourself is bad for you. That's crazy. You don't have to do crazy things to get the help you need.

Krys stopped slashing herself very soon after that. She did so only once more and that was a tiny scratch. Getting rid of most of the sick Parent messages and building in healthy ones took several months. After that she gradually learned to recognize and cut off any forms of craziness very quickly. That was several years ago. Her life has never been the same since. During the process of her therapy she became very dependent for a time. However, she is now a well-functioning and autonomous woman.

JOY

A letter came from overseas. It was from Joy asking if she could come for three months' extensive therapy with me. She explained that her local therapist suggested she come. Joy had a long history of emotional problems and had been hospitalized twice some time ago; she had been on medication since then, and most recently had become suicidal.

Upon the recommendation of the same therapist, she had attended a seminar I conducted in her country a few months before. My response to her after she told me that her life was not worth living had made a profound impression upon her. I had said something like "It's good that you are alive. There's a reason for you being here. You can find out what you need to do to have a good life. Go to it!"

Joy allowed those words to give her permission and encouragement to deal with her issues. Although she had made a no-suicide contract with her therapist some weeks before the seminar, she had not taken the necessary steps to decide to live—and to live fully. Now she was ready to deal with her issues...and so she came.

Joy's Story

I always had a feeling of not being good enough, regardless of what I did. I was the oldest and felt that my brother and sister always overshadowed me. They were bright, intelligent, pretty, able to draw, and I never quite measured up to them. I married at twenty because I wanted to be loved. But my husband proved to be violent. After four years of marriage and two nervous breakdowns I separated from him. I returned to work to support myself and my two-year-old son.

One day when I went to pick up my son from the nursery, I found my husband had taken him without my permission. A court case regarding custody ensued, and my husband was given custody. I was given access only one weekend each month. Heartbroken over the loss of my child, I decided to take an overseas trip to try to forget my hurts. During this time my husband filed for divorce; I fought the divorce but lost, and my husband continued to have custody of my son.

When it was time for my son to visit, I thought about his departure from the time he arrived, and so was not able to enjoy the short times I had with him. I also felt guilty over my broken marriage because of my religious beliefs. I had never considered the possibility that some marriages might just be impossible.

When I started therapy I had a deep sense of guilt and unworthiness. I was working full time, going to adult education classes, keeping busy every minute to try to block out the past, and very depressed. I had no one to turn to. I believed that I would never make a "go of life." I had failed at marriage and felt there was no future for me. Life was not worth living. No one wanted me. I thought the only solution was to go insane or to die. At least if I went insane I wouldn't be aware of what was going on in life. However, deep down I knew that neither of these courses was an answer to my problems. I still had a strong faith that God did exist, although I questioned why things happened to me. I concluded I must have been really bad to deserve my situation. During my marriage I had some counseling at a marriage guidance center. When I was hospitalized I was given medication. My local physician was helpful and I also saw various psychiatrists, all of whom insisted on medication. I discussed my problems with various Christian ministers and continued to pray.

Some time after my divorce I sought help from another counselor who eventually suggested I attend the seminar one of the authors was conducting while she was in Australia. I found the seminar helpful. He suggested that I go to the United States and do some intensive work with her there.

My therapy with this therapist was intense. She did not require that I take medication. This time I was far away from my situations and familiar surroundings. There was no pressure to conform to what was expected by others. It was a new world and became a new beginning. I related better to my new therapist than to any of my previous therapists. Perhaps this was because she was a woman, and I had previously always had male therapists. I felt I was accepted by the other people I met in her groups, as well as by my therapist. I gained a greater awareness of other people who had also experienced problems with their feelings. Coming to the realization that I was not the only one was very significant for me. A man in our group who was getting divorced at the time was very upset. By being with him and seeing his anguish I came to realize that I was not strange for having felt sad and depressed.

During my therapy I came to realize that I needed to go beyond my contract not to kill myself. I needed to decide I was going to live life. I came to realize there is life after the death of a marriage, and failing at one thing did not mean I must fail at everything. The failure of my marriage was not all my fault. I am OK even when I do not feel OK. I do many things well; I am not strange because I feel; I can have a good life despite the past.

My first stage in therapy was allowing myself to be aware of my feelings rather than rejecting them or trying to push them away. I found I could pinpoint times of difficulty, re-experience my feelings of inadequacy, depression, anger, and anxiety, and work through them. I came to see how I had been confusing feelings and thinking. For example, instead of allowing myself to feel sad and express my sadness I focused on telling myself what a failure I had been. As a result, I felt worse and worse, but still had not allowed myself to express my sadness and get over it.

In another stage of therapy I observed how other people who had similar feelings to mine were able to work through their problems. I came to know that I could be OK and accepted, and I overcame my fear of rejection and failure.

In a major stage I pinpointed my ex-husband's hold on me—he was like a rope binding me so that I was unable to do anything without his approval. I came to terms with that restriction. I got rid of the rope and began to exert myself. I came to know the freedom of being myself rather than bound by others. I came to know that I was OK despite my broken marriage and any other mistakes I had made. I could rebuild my life.

After my three months of an in-depth psychotherapy I continued my overseas trip feeling free! I prayed that I would find a future husband. On my return to Australia I moved to another city away from my parents permanently. I gave myself the freedom to fall in love and the courage to marry twelve months later. I no longer need to keep myself busy all the time in an attempt to block out the past. I now do many things for enjoyment: bread making, crafts, Bible study, cooking, and even working part time.

My son came to live with us for five years during his university education. I enjoy looking after my husband and do not feel constrained by him or by being married. I am involved in a church missionary organization which meets in our home; I participate in fund-raising events; I joined a concert group that sings in older peoples' homes; I have enough free time to be and to do things I enjoy. And after fourteen years my marriage is still an asset to me, instead of a liability.

Having read Joy's story, you will understand that I hesitate to tell people how long they will need to be in therapy. Many people who have had a history of emotional problems similar to Joy's would take much longer to make the kind of changes she did. As Goethe says:

There is one elementary *truth*—
the ignorance of which kills countless ideas and splendid plans. The moment one definitely commits oneself, then Providence moves too. All sorts of things occur to help one that never otherwise would have occurred...
Whatever you can do.
Or dream you can do.
Begin it.
Boldness has genius, power and magic in it.
Begin it now.

Joy decided she was coming here to solve her problems. She determined she would find meaning for her life. She had three months to do it, was willing to give it her best, and found that all sorts of unexpected doors did open for her.

Relationship Problems

CONNIE

When I first saw Connie, a sister in a religious order, it was as if I had just encountered a little child who was hiding and yet peeping to see if it was safe to let me know she was there. As she began to tell her story I could understand how living in her house must have been very scary for a tiny child. Now, in her late thirties, Connie was still a frightened little girl inside. She spoke with a very soft voice and her face looked much younger than her years. However, she had a distinctive and determined walk with long and measured strides.

The daughter of alcoholic and abusive parents, Connie learned very early that the safest thing to do was to attempt to figure out what other people wanted. Often this was to hide and stay out of the way. She was never supposed to have any needs of her own but she was always expected to be responsible, to be perfect, and to please others all the time. By the time she began therapy, most of her energy was being used to figure out what she thought other people wanted her to do. She was completely out of touch with her own needs. She was trying to please everyone else and felt rejected, hopeless, and unloved when her efforts were unappreciated. She had so denied her own sense of identity that it was as if she were fading into the woodwork. Her hair, skin, and clothes were almost the same color.

Having had a little therapy in another town, Connie knew she wanted group therapy. Mostly she wanted to overcome her sense of hopelessness and her belief that the world would be a better place if she were not alive. She also wanted to be able to have friends, to know she was lovable, and to develop a sense of identity. As she left my office on that first day with her head down, I was glad she had those deliberate strides. It was as if her feet were saying, "I will, I will, I will."

Connie's Story

When I came to therapy I had only a vague sense of what I needed. I knew that I exhibited symptoms of anxiety. I was also aware that I was not happy with friends. I was rarely treated the way I wanted to be treated. I knew part of the problem was that I was seeking a mother rather than a peer. I also knew that my family life and experiences as a child were affecting me as an adult. But I was so protected by denial and self-blindness that I had very little insight into what was wrong. Actually, I had a gnawing sensation deep inside of me that I was not yet really a person. I hoped that I could indeed become "real."

To a stranger my family would have seemed to be a fairly good one, except that my parents drank too much. Both were gentle and loving and had a sense of responsibility. My mother was often too responsible. Yet, there was another side to their personalities. It was as if they changed into different people when they were at home and the doors were shut. My mother especially showed little stability and easily became a senselessly cruel tyrant. She was as cruel in this state as she was volatile.

Both of my parents beat me frequently for childish faults such as forgetting and not knowing. (I had no way of knowing, since I was only a little child.) Neither one seemed to realize that a child is not born with infused knowledge, as well as social and work skills. Their verbal abuse was painful to me. Mom often told me I was no good and she wished I had never been born. Indeed, she had taken lye when she was pregnant with me. She said it was because Dad wanted her to drink and she did not want to drink while she was pregnant! Dad's verbal abuse consisted of deriding me and making me give in to my little sister, who was four years younger than I. For a period of about three years he rarely spoke to me at all.

My parents were violent toward one another. Twice they knocked over our Christmas tree while in physical combat. Once they were fighting so hard that my sister and I were sure only one of them would come out alive.

When I was eight my father asked me to have sex with him. I had no idea of the implications, but I sensed it was something we should not be doing. I wanted nothing more than to please him and Mom, so it was hard for me even to hesitate. Even though I had begun to realize that Mom was in need of me to care for her, I still looked up to her as the beacon of goodness. I asked if she would do what Dad wanted, and when she said yes, I complied with no hesitation at all. I actually enjoyed the experience so much that I could hardly wait to share it with Mom. The look in her eyes when I told her of the "fun thing" Dad and I had done last night changed my life—changed me forever.

Actually, I was never a child after the age of two. I was expected to be more grown up than my parents. I perceived my mother as a child. I saw her crying in rage at my grandmother and realized she had never "grown up."

One day when I was about six she took me to a movie. When I told her I needed to go to the restroom, she did not take me because it was an interesting part of the movie. I tried hard not to but I wet my pants, including my thick winter leggings. When she took me to the restroom and draped my wet leggings over the radiator to dry she cried. I felt so miserable I determined I would *never* be any trouble to her again. I tried to take care of her in every way, but she would not be pleased or accept love and care from anyone, let alone the clumsy efforts of a little child.

The fact that I could not please my parents resulted in my feeling like a total failure. I felt as if there was no good in me. I was convinced I was evil, even as bad as the devil. I thought perhaps I *was* the devil. I felt as if I was made of rock inside. I could not eat. I contemplated suicide at the age of nine, but I was afraid I would go to hell. Deep inside, in spite of all my despair, I felt that I might get better if I just tried harder. Although I tried I could not swallow, and I hid my food so as not to upset Mom. By the time this was discovered I was in danger of irreversible damage. I had to stay in bed for six weeks. Both parents treated me as a child during this time. This is the only time in my childhood I felt safe and loved.

When I was eleven I knew I could not go on with the emptiness and lack of purpose that still made me feel like a rock inside. I prayed for help and began to go to church. This helped me very much. Through religion I began to learn to make my own decisions. I found great love and strength in Jesus and his holy mother. I also acquired some new problems from an over-emphasis on sin and a misunderstanding of what forgiveness means. I thought that by completely denying my feelings I would be fine. I did not realize how much anger I had repressed.

Religion was one of the ways I kept myself functional, but in my late thirties, the false facades and defenses I had built around and about myself with the help of religion had crumbled. I felt as if I were on very shaky ground. The muscles in my throat tightened and I had spasms. I was given Valium. One of my problems was grief and the surfacing anger I carried against my mother who had died a few years ago. My best friend died just three weeks before my mother. Because of all my unresolved anger I had not resolved my grief. My other methods of survival had been self-discipline and people pleasing.

I carried all of this with me when I started therapy. Initially I had one session with a psychiatrist who said I had identified my anger with my mother. He said he was sure I could work it out. If I thought I needed help, he recommended group therapy. I joined a group and that helped. Then I was transferred and after some searching I found out about one of the authors of this book and asked if I could join one of her groups.

Although my former group experience had been helpful, the therapist challenged me so directly and harshly that I felt assaulted and even wounded. My new therapist confronted me, too, but never in a way to belittle my dignity or my values. Instead she worked to strengthen them.

In recognition of my lack of nurturing as a child, my therapist gave me the opportunity to experience some of the parenting I had always craved. First she held me as if I were six months old and I didn't need to do anything except be there and enjoy. I remember this as a wonderful feeling of being loved and cared for with no strings. The other group members were also gentle and loving toward me. I remember this time with peace and I am still able to nurture myself with these thoughts when I need it.

Some time later, and when I was ready, I did some more "little work" in group. This time I was two years old and I said no because that's what I wanted to say, and it felt so good!

Still later I was four. We had several group members being little and being cared for according to their needs. One of them was also four. What fun! We were not too good at sharing or politeness. We often wanted to play with the same toy, and our therapist needed to set limits for us. I profited from this very much. I began to feel that it was good that I was alive and that I had rights and could ask to have them met. I experienced discipline without battering; that was new and very healing.

Another series of exercises that was very helpful for me was that of expressing and experiencing not only anger but my enormous rage. The exercise that gave me the most insight into this was one in which I was held down and had to get people off my back. I was furious. The people on my back represented the messages I was still carrying around in my head and which told me, "I am bad," "I am in the way," "People are better off without me," and "I can never do enough," or "I can never do it right." My therapist told me to get out from under them. I did it! It took five people to hold me and they were not able to keep me down. I felt exhilarated and relieved—like a new person ready and with room in my head to take in new messages about belonging, being worthwhile, and my best being good enough. I realized this exercise was more than a symbol. I was no longer bound by those terrible burdens.

My therapist's love, caring, and respect for me generated a feeling of acceptance of my self-worth. This was reinforced by other therapists who joined her for special workshops from time to time. One was the other author of this book. I felt accepted by each of these people and the others in my group. This also contributed much to my growth.

My achievement of personhood has been clearly marked by phases, each of these ongoing rather than done; it was a spiral rather than a straight line with a beginning and an end. At first, the changes were very large and major; now, I am dealing with insights that enhance my ability to love myself and others.

My first stage was the blind or vague phase. I recognized something was awry, but had no concept of the part I was playing in setting up conditions that produced discomfort or lack of good feelings. Next came a facing-the-truth or awareness phase, in which I began to see and understand my own part in setting up conditions for unhappiness. This was a traumatic and painful experience as well as a crucial time when I had to decide to go on or get stuck in the mire of personal helplessness and lack of responsibility.

The third phase was one of conversion or changing of attitude. During this time I learned how to change my thought processes and attitudes. I began to feel my feelings and I made specific behavior changes. Finally came the enjoyment phase, in which I basked in positive payoffs resulting from my own positive choices. This was often accompanied by warm and exhilarating changes in other people's responses to me.

The major change I made is that I took responsibility for my own life and happiness. I stopped trying to be perfect. I accepted myself as lovable and a worthwhile human being. I now am able to give and receive love in ways I had never known before. I now accept love and friendship on the terms that the other person is able to give it. I no longer require that people prove they love me. I now enjoy and appreciate friendship from every quarter. I acknowledge good and positive things which before I discounted or did not even notice. Before my therapy I had many problems in relating to the Sisters with whom I lived; now I am very happy while living with several other sisters. In short, I am a happy, loved, and loving person.

Revisiting my past was not always easy, but it had great rewards. My faith in God has played an important part in my getting over seemingly impossible hurdles. I also recognize the value and help I have had from healthy friends. Now that I am healthy I play a part in helping others to have the courage to change and accept themselves.

When children have unmet needs, they often learn to survive by developing a magical thinking system and adapting their behavior to fit in with their beliefs. When Connie was tiny she realized she was not loved or wanted. She decided the reason she was not loved was that she was too demanding and not helpful enough. She determined that when she was good enough, helpful enough, and no bother to anyone, her mother would love her. However, no matter how helpful she was she did not find the love she sought.

Turning to the church and the faith she developed helped Connie a great deal. She knew God loved her and she came to believe there was a purpose to her living. However, she was still operating from her magical belief that in order to be loved or accepted by other people she had to be nothing but helpful and stay out of the way. She believed her own needs were not important, yet she felt isolated and depressed when she was not accepted by others.

Connie had amazing strength, yet felt helpless. She had survived an attempted abortion, not being wanted or loved, the hazards and unpredictabilities of growing up with two alcoholic parents, and sexual abuse. The only sense of security she had was her faith, but even now this began to crumble. She had focused so much on being sinful that she had been unable to incorporate the meaning of redemption and forgiveness.

"Little work" (see Part Two) was an important part of Connie's therapy. Once she knew she was loved, she began to glow and no longer needed to hide. Only when she began to get in touch with her power—beginning by saying, "No!" and then getting all of those burdens off her back—did she feel safe to become aware of and express her anger. Once she dealt with her anger she made redecisions about herself and her world. Then she was able to forgive her parents, herself, and others who had misunderstood her. Since then she has gone from strength to strength.

DANA

I looked out of my window shortly before Dana was due for her first appointment. I saw a young woman walking very slowly, with her head down and as if she had no energy. I had just spent an hour with a woman who was very depressed, withdrawn, and distant, and I said to myself, "It looks as if I have two withdrawn ones in a row today." I could not have been further from the mark. Once in my office Dana was a ball of energy and anything but withdrawn.

She presented herself with an air of assurance. She was attractive, verbal, and friendly, but she had become an expert in hiding her pain and inner torture from others. She was aware that she had decided at an early age that she would never trust men. Now she was at the point of wondering if she would ever trust anyone—even herself.

Dana's Story

I entered therapy when I realized that my inability to become and stay close to others who were important to me was a problem which I felt I could not solve alone. At the time, I identified myself as a "radical lesbian separatist." I meant that I wanted to be close only to women, and yet my relationships with women were besieged by the very same problems which had destroyed my relationships with men.

Another motivation for me to seek help was my troublesome career situation. While I had trained as a classical musician, I was barely able to eke out a living at it. Although music was something I had been programmed to do from an early age, I found myself enjoying it less and less.

I had attempted to mask or ease the discomfort I felt by attending church, talking to a college counselor, smoking marijuana, joining a lesbian support group and exploring "women's spirituality," and celebrating nature through paganism.

When I began therapy I was angry most of the time without acknowledging it. I projected a "strong front." I acted as one who could handle everything all on her own, although that was far from the truth. I enjoyed shocking people with outrageous behavior or by doing the unexpected. I learned later that this was my way of keeping my distance from others. For example, I enjoyed holding hands in public with a girlfriend not primarily because of the closeness but because of the discomfort it would cause others. At one point I even shaved my head. My life to this point had been one of extremes. The thought of balance stirred the fear of boredom in me. Staying at one extreme or another meant that I would at least feel something, even if it were just excitement.

I let no one in. My feelings of self-worth were nearly nonexistent; if I let another too close that person would surely see what I saw when I looked at myself—someone not worth loving. So I kept others at arm's length and settled for the excitement of an unpredictable life. The irony was that my life became quite predictable as relationship after relationship took on the same pattern of desire followed by distance.

My low self-worth was rooted in my youth as an only child of alcoholic parents in a dysfunctional marriage. I still smile today when I see a magazine cover warning of the dangers of divorce. I used to pray secretly that my parents would divorce. My reaction to their frequent and vicious arguments was to assume the role of negotiator. This inevitably ended in disaster. I didn't understand then, as I do now, that they chose to drink, to argue, and sometimes to abuse each other physically because they wanted a confirmation of their belief that the world is a cruel place where no one can be trusted.

During therapy, I began to understand that I had copied the best and the worst qualities of my parents—my mother's intense energy and fire along with her obsessiveness and vindictiveness, and my father's intelligence and curiosity along with his coldness and fear of emotional intimacy.

I grew up "knowing" that men were superior to women. Both my parents' behavior confirmed this, albeit in unusual ways. My mother demonstrated it by being extremely competitive...and what else was she trying to prove than her own worth? My father demonstrated the myth of male superiority by withdrawing each time I or my mother faced him with an emotion, whether it was happiness, fear, sorrow, or anger. On the rare occasions he chose not to withdraw, fights inevitably followed.

I took on the competitiveness—I was driven to be "the best." Best at what was not important; as long as I was better than everyone else I was all right. "Win/win" was a startling and new concept to me when it was introduced in therapy. After all, what was the challenge if someone else could win too? Being "the best" was more than just a challenge. It was the only way I felt that I deserved some crumbs of love. If I suffered in order to become "the best," and if I stepped over all the others to emerge at the top, then I was okay for awhile. It was never okay to rest for too long. The concept of unconditional love which was introduced in my therapy was the single most influential factor in the changes which I made then and in the changes I have made since. Imagine my surprise at "being enough" or being "just right" without having to do anything! Needless to say these messages took some time to sink in.

When I first entered therapy, I spent most of my time being judgmental of the other people in my group. This was one of the most perfected distancing techniques I had. This also allowed me to focus my energy on others instead of doing any real work on myself. While others worked in our group, I silently criticized them in my head. How could they be so stupid? So obvious? So neurotic? I was telling myself I was superior. They couldn't possibly relate to a lesbian anyway—why bother making any emotional investment in them?

Over time I began to feel somewhat safer—safe enough to take some risks. The way I rationalized this to myself was, "If they're all making such fools of themselves, they are not going to notice me doing the same...so why not give it a try?" It is ironic that I perceived myself as being so daring! I remember one session where I unloaded what felt like a dump truck full of anger at my parents. I beat pillows and screamed until I was exhausted, and then it came out...that intense pain hiding behind my anger for so many years. Waves of hurt swept over and out of me as I sobbed from the deepest part of me. I worked with these feelings for weeks afterwards, and slowly began to replace my mistaken beliefs about myself and the world with new beliefs filled with love and assurance.

Following this, I began a slow process of forgiving my parents. This process was completed only recently. After seeing how I had shaped my past I began to believe I could create my future. I began to see possibilities for my life that I had never considered before. They began as belief statements like "I deserve to be happy" and evolved into behavior changes like going back to school in a new career field. At the same time, I let go of some of the harsher judgments I had of others, and allowed a few people to get close to me. I allowed myself to receive the friendship, the warmth, and the love of those special people.

About a year after I finished therapy, I met and fell in love with a man who is now my husband. We have two beautiful children. I have a satisfying career as a manager in a large corporation, and have most recently been developing and leading personal growth workshops. I view my own personal and spiritual growth as something that is ongoing and will continue throughout my life. Some of my best moments in this regard are my sessions with myself after a workshop. During this time I apply to myself the principles and exercises of the workshop I have just facilitated for others. I weep (usually for joy), I write down my insights in a journal, and feel a strong connection to myself, to others and to God.[1]

Like so many people who conceal their pain from others and who develop convincing facades, Dana's major problem was not

---

[1] It is important to point out there are many, many women who are lesbians who are healthy and well-balanced. I just was not one of them. I don't believe there is any relationship between mental/emotional health and sexual preference. I don't want it to sound like I was confused, and therefore gay, and then became clear, and therefore straight. It does not always work that way and is certainly not that simple.

at all what she feared. She believed she was unlovable and there-fore feared that if she allowed anyone to get close to her that per-son would discover her secret, believe it, and abandon her. The real problem was that what she believed was not true. She had built a carefully executed plan on an assumption that was false.

No wonder Dana was so angry. Because she believed she was unlovable she felt hopeless and empty. Her earliest memories were all very scary, although for many years she had been able to repress much of her trauma and fear. For as long as she could re-member she had been encouraged to perform, to excel, to be bet-ter than other children and to be the top of the heap. She had done that superbly. She was a brilliant musician both as a per-former and as a teacher. When I met her in her early twenties, she held a position not generally assigned to anyone under forty.

She'd achieved much, but her sense of emptiness and futility remained. All of her achievements were beginning to lose the power she had once thought they would have to make her feel like a worthwhile person.

One day in group therapy she told of longing when she was lit-tle for her father to love her. Apparently he only noticed her when he did not like what she was doing. At one time—probably when he was annoyed—he had said, "Why don't you go and get lost in the traffic?" Being a normal, literal three year old, she decided to do just that. Her family lived on a busy boulevard and she crossed one street and found shelter in the midway. She felt con-fused and scared. She was there for what seemed an eternity. The traffic became heavier and louder and more terrifying. She kept on thinking, "He'll come and get me," but he did not come. Final-ly, a stranger noticed her and took her home.

When I asked her what she decided about herself that day, she said, "Even when I do what he says he doesn't want me. I must be bad, and no one will ever love me." She also recalled learning lat-er the figurative meaning of "Get lost in the traffic" and the awful pain she experienced when she knew for sure that he had never wanted her.

In therapy Dana realized how it made sense to reach those de-cisions at that time in her life and how at age three she was not able to do anything about her father's issues. She had no choice about growing up with her parents with their particular sets of problems. However, she could make new decisions about its being good that she is here, that she is lovable, and that she is wanted now.

Not long after her redecision work Dana gradually learned how to become her own best friend. She strengthened her beliefs in herself to the point that those beliefs moved from the level of belief to that of real knowledge. Now she knew she could trust herself.

The following week Dana wanted to do some more work in relation to her father. She returned to the same memory and one or two others when he had been mean to her. This time she said that she had felt so scared around him that she had decided that all men were mean and she would never trust one again. Now she realized that the fact was he was mean, and that said nothing about all the other men in the world. She told each of the men in the group that she trusted them and asked one if she could sit by him and have him put his arm around her shoulder.

I knew at that moment that she was no longer a separatist and she had a psychological freedom she had never known before.

LINDA

At our first interview Linda's message to me was, "I'm a tough nut to crack." She was sure no one could help her. Her life was empty and lonely. She felt abandoned, isolated, and hopeless.

What Linda did not know was that I would make no effort to crack her shell. Instead I'd do all to expose the "tough nut" to optimum conditions for growth from the inside, so that Linda's own exploration would do that for her. When I suggested she'd be most likely to solve her problems with the support and challenge group therapy would provide, she was not exactly enthusiastic about the idea but was willing to commit herself to come for two months. We agreed that, at the end of that time, she would decide whether to keep on with the group, change to individual therapy, or terminate.

Linda's Story
(Part One)

When I was in my late thirties I was in a lot of psychological pain that would not go away. My husband had left me several years before and I was struggling financially and against my ex-husband's undermining behavior to raise my children alone.

Divorce carried a large social stigma. All of my friends were married and few knew what to do with me. I was attractive and some women thought I would "steal" their husbands. I had no brothers or sisters and my mother smothered me, wanting to take charge of my children, my house, and me. My parents believed a woman alone was helpless and powerless. I often felt guilty when I made decisions about my own life without their permission.

After my divorce I dated many men. Then I met the love of my life. He was a tall, dark, and handsome surgeon who had never been married. We shared friends, a sense of humor, love of life, and common interests. We were both Jewish and we loved being together. We shared thoughts and feelings and often spoke of marriage although a date was never mentioned. After many months he telephoned to tell me he was not going to see me any more. He said he was too much in love with me, and could not marry me because I had two children. He had known about my children from the day we met.

I was crushed, sad, angry, and overwhelmed with grief. My grief would not go away, no matter how busy I kept. There was a constant ache in my heart. I was depressed and had no idea of what do do about it. My closest friend, who had been divorced and remarried, was seeing you and being helped. When I came to see you I was secretly hoping you would give me the magic wand to get my boyfriend back.

I was somewhat skeptical of coming to you. I did not know what to expect. When I was a young child my mother had sought help from a counselor for a major problem that never got resolved and affected our household for life. After my divorce I sought help from a psychiatrist. I did gain some coping skills but I never really felt well. There were times when I took prescribed tranquilizers as well as sleeping pills.

When I broke up with my surgeon friend, I spoke with my family and friends and I was told, "Time heals all wounds." They knew I could "tough it out." I found this platitude neither caring or true and maintained a level of chronic depression until I came into therapy.

From the moment I entered the office on that first day, I was nervous and was asking myself, "Why am I here? Why am I wasting my time? Therapy won't make any difference." I was scared, but the therapist's reassuring, quiet, gentleness helped put me at ease. I wanted the magic to bring my friend back. I wanted her to remove my pain and make me feel better. When she recommended group therapy, I was reluctant, but agreed to try it.

I entered a group, thinking I was different from all the others. They needed help, while I had only one problem. When I shared why I was there, my therapist asked how I felt about what I was saying. This was new for me. As I listened to the others, I knew I'd found something I'd never experienced before.

Gradually I realized that my feelings had been minimized and ignored when I was a child. I had been told my feelings were wrong, or that I was "crazy" to feel what I felt. The therapist and group confronted my false belief system. I was prodded to learn to recognize and express my feelings. This was very difficult at first. She provided many safe vehicles for me to express my feelings, like pounding a pillow to get anger out of my system rather than keeping on talking about it. It was helpful for me to learn how to deal with inner turmoil by having the two conflicting parts of me dialogue with each other. Learning about Transactional Analysis helped me to understand my own Parent, Adult, and Child, as well as to communicate with others. I learned to use my own power, rather than stay helpless and hopeless.

For the first time in my life I began to experience love and caring without judgment. I learned to understand others. I formed many friendships in the group and we met and had fun together in other settings. I am still in touch with some of those people, years later. I could count on the others in our group to confront me, challenge me, love me, and support me.

I learned at a fundamental level to accept my own uniqueness, with all of my personal assets and liabilities. I learned to ask clearly for what I wanted and needed, whether it be support, strokes, or anything else. I tapped into my personal power and intelligence and acknowledged how special and dynamic I am. I learned to take risks to achieve my goals and to visualize myself achieving what I wanted. I learned to express my disappointment in others and to forgive them for their shortcomings. I learned how to let go of non-productive thoughts and feelings. Learning that what we were taught when we were young still influences us today freed me to re-decide my future. Little by little I began to integrate what I learned, and today it is an integral part of me.

I will always remember walking into group therapy one night when I had not been a member for very long. I announced that I needed major surgery that would save my life, and that I had decided not to have it because I did not want to go through the experience as a single person and with my out-of-town physician. My therapist and colleague took me seriously and helped me work through my intense fear and anger until I decided to have the surgery. By the time of my hospitalization I had learned to believe in my own strength and that I was worth staying alive.

Group therapy gave me a role model for new behaviors. Change does not occur when people are afraid to abandon the familiar, and therefore continue to do what they have always done. Group therapy offers a safe environment in which to accomplish this.

I entered therapy knowing I was bright and attractive. Deep inside I felt like a failure and was sad, but I stayed unaware or denied my feelings in an attempt to ease my pain. The first stage of my therapy was loosening up my resistance. Initially I resisted any change even if I thought I wanted it; I had no idea how I could still be me if I changed, nor did I know how to change. My resistance decreased a bit at a time as I tried new behaviors in the group. The thought of being successful was exciting and particularly threatening to me. I'd been told so often, "You can't," "You don't count," "You're crazy," that I believed those things.

At my next stage I ventured into some risk taking as I gained confidence and began to believe in myself more and more. With risks came success and increasing belief in myself. With positive experiences to draw on, I began to take charge of my household as I wanted it to be. I allowed my parents to influence me less and less.

For a while I went through a phase of having a "laundry list" of problems, and thinking that when each of them was solved my life would be just right. Then I realized it was up to me to learn the skills to deal with any situation, and I became open to new ideas.

Therapy changed my life in many ways. The most poignant memory that I hold is still a mystery to me. I entered the hospital for surgery with an anticipated stay of two weeks. Everything that could go wrong did. I remained there for ten weeks and had three major surgeries. A day after the second surgery, still groggy from the anesthesia, my lungs began to fill with fluid. I told myself I could let myself die or endure the pain of coughing to clear my lungs. I cleared my lungs, thus choosing life. I returned to my nursing education and from that point on received straight A's for the next two years and then throughout graduate school. Prior to that point, although I was bright, I had struggled for average grades. I learned that whatever I decided to achieve I could do. Subsequently, I've won many awards. The bottom line of therapy has been that I've learned to believe in myself. I can express my thoughts and feelings freely, although I still need to be careful to do that in a non-threatening way. Owning what I think and feel, I do not need others to agree with me, although I still like them to respect my position. I've achieved greater love and intimacy with others. I've learned to read, understand, and accept others for who they are. I've counseled others and am very good at what I do.

I ended my therapy with a renewed ability to set goals and focus my life on achieving them. I have remarried and have been able to help my husband express his feelings. I've taught college and counseled my students. I have an expertise in the area of grief and loss and have published in professional journals.

Therapy, because it was at such a deep level, allowed me to receive new messages about who I am. I am a worthwhile, loving, and lovable woman. I received new Parent messages along with the nurturing I did not receive from my own parents. I was able to separate from my parents, forgive them for hurting me, and accept them for who they are. I am truly blessed by this, for I am able to have a good relationship with them in their older years.

Linda's Story
(Part Two)

Some time after I had left group and two years after my ten-week hospitalization, I began to experience a worsening pain on one side of my body and around the incisions. I was unable to raise my arm high or to wear any tight clothing around my waist. When I began nurse's training on the hospital wards, the attacks of pain were unbearable. It took almost a year for the doctors to diagnose that the pain was being caused by nerves that had been torn during surgery. After a year of painful injection therapy with poor results, I underwent two more surgeries to sever nerves at the spinal cord and to rebuild my incision. There was about an 80 percent improvement, but I was still uncomfortable. My neurosurgeon suggested I try hypnosis and move my pain to another part of my body. I called my therapist, although she had never worked with anyone with this type of pain. She said she would not recommend attempting to transfer my pain to another part of my body because it would still be with me. She contracted to teach me how to do self-hypnosis and to develop a program to get rid of the pain altogether.

We met weekly and worked through progressive relaxation techniques. I practiced daily, slipped into a hypnotic state, and gave myself new messages. I also learned to visualize moving my body freely and without pain. I learned to be aware of how my other arm felt as I reached upwards with it and then imagined moving my painful arm and having it feel the same way. I gradually practiced actually moving it like that until I could do it without pain. Sometimes I resisted, but I stuck with it until my resistance passed. After several weeks I was pain-free and have been ever since. My hypno-therapy truly made me a physically active person again.

It is clear to me both as a patient and as a nurse that coping with the limitations, anger, fear, sadness, hopelessness, and helplessness of chronic illness is almost impossible without counseling. I had been diagnosed with kidney disease and had my first kidney operation at age seventeen. The surgery was not done properly, and a year later the surgeon died. The operation had been done as an emergency and we were not aware that the chairman of the department was a tenured alcoholic.

My disease progressed over the next ten years until I found an outstanding urologist who reoperated successfully. Many times I felt very lonely; support groups did not exist then, nor did I know anyone with chronic illness. I lived disease-free for seven years until I discovered that my other kidney was being affected. The surgeon I trusted lived out of state, and it was at this point that I came to my group not wanting to deal with the whole problem. Being hospitalized out of state was very lonely since only my family came to visit. However, the support, calls, and cards I had from you and my group played a big part in helping me to keep going.

By the time I had my pain-reducing surgeries, I had had enough group therapy to know how to tell people my feelings. This is very important with physicians and nurses. I remember nurses yelling at me because my blood pressure had gone down close to zero and they had become frightened. One nurse was nasty when I asked what was in an injection. I am highly allergic to several things, and I have learned how important it is to share this information and thus be a responsible partner with physicians and nurses.

I remember that many times I would have liked to run away and avoid my negative feelings, but it was by facing the pain and my feelings that I found the strength to change. I continue to use this skill whenever I am faced with painful situations. In all my experience I have never met anyone who had learned the coping skills needed for long-term illness until they were in the situation, and they all needed outside help to do that. People are physically healthier when they deal with their feelings.

I will continue to grow all my life, as that is important to me. I know I could call my old therapist or any of my group friends at any time and ask for what I want. There has been an understanding with them that I have not had with other friends. I have not felt sorry for myself. I am proud of how I cope. I am a richer person for having had the courage to seek help when I could no longer deal with my conflicts on my own. It has been a process worth its weight in gold.

Linda not only gained the strength to come out of her shell, but also allowed herself to grow. Initially everything she experienced in group was so different from anything she had known before that she was amazed beyond belief. As she says, she had convinced herself that she was not expected to feel, and if she did she certainly was not supposed to tell anyone about it. I will never forget her eyes during those first few weeks. She has big eyes naturally, but when she was scared they seemed to look twice their size.

Initially she was highly defensive and thought she was different from anyone else in the group. This looked as if she thought she was superior. However, the reality was that she felt quite inadequate. One of the dramatic changes that everyone noticed was that as Linda began to accept herself and gradually come out of her shell she became warmer and warmer to everyone else in the group.

Linda had serious setbacks from time to time, but despite the temptation to revert to her hopelessness she allowed herself to trust enough to go through everything that was needed physically and psychologically, after beginning to enjoy good health. Then she grew and blossomed beautifully.

Three Young Children

TIMOTHY

Timothy was four. Not only was he clinging to his mother when she brought him to see me, but he was hiding his face in her skirt. For the past several days he had been waking up screaming in the middle of the night, following his parents around the house, and clinging with both arms whenever he was taken out of the house.

CHRISTINE

Christine was three when I first met her. She had started wetting her bed at night and having accidents during the day. She was not manifesting any other symptoms. She entered my office holding her mother's hand, but let her hand go and moved quickly to pick up and hold on to one of the bears that sat waiting on the davenport where she would sit. She was all smiles.

NICHOLE

Nichole is Christine's big sister. She was four and a half when her mother brought both girls to see me. Nichole was having stomachaches and bad dreams. As she entered the room, her eyes were focused on me as if she were sizing me up and down. She stopped looking long enough to see a clown with the toys and decided to take it and sit on the other side of her mother. She held the clown very tight and talked fast.

All three children were anxious and were afraid that some terrible thing was going to happen. When adults are anxious, it is important for them to feel as if they have something they can hold on to. Children do this naturally. If they are not holding on to a person, they will embrace a toy.

Timothy's Story
(Told by his mother)

Timothy had always been an easygoing and happy child. Nothing seemed to bother him. One day in kindergarten a child there told him that the father of one of their classmates, Mary, had been shot dead. Someone had put a gun to the back of his head. The teacher knew that many of the children had heard about the murder; it had been widely publicized in the papers, radio, and television, and some parents had told her that their children knew about it. Later the teacher told the children what had happened and explained that that was why Mary was away that day. The teacher prayed for the man and his family with the class and asked all of the children to be particularly kind to Mary when she returned to kindergarten.

Timothy showed no immediate reaction, but a few days later he began clinging to his father and to me. We asked him if anything was wrong and he declared that everything was fine. But everything was not fine and he started clinging more and more. As long as he was at home with at least one of us he showed no signs of distress, although he did want to be in the same room we were in more than he had in the past. He especially did not want to go to kindergarten, and he put on a terrible scene each morning. He'd cling, cry, and plead with me not to leave him. When I left, he settled down with his teacher after a time, but the next day it was the same all over again. He had always liked to go to the neighbors, but now he refused to go unless one of us was with him.

We tried talking to him, gentle persuasion, reasoning, and making him separate from us, but nothing worked. He even clung to my arm throughout a birthday party. He finally told us he was convinced that if he let both of us out of his sight, one or the other of us would never come home again. We told him that if we left we would always tell when we'd be back. We felt we could not promise him that we would never have an accident; although the probabilities were slim we could not say that would never happen to us.

He'd go to sleep all right, but then he'd wake up during the night and want to get into our bed. One of us would get up and lie down in his room until he fell off to sleep again. This continued night after night. The rest of his behavior was just fine, and he kept his good appetite throughout the ordeal.

We had an Employee Assistance Program at work through which we could get counseling for any kind of crisis. I called the headquarters and was referred to one of the authors. We came for three visits. The first one was just for half an hour, when the therapist talked to Timothy and started to get to know him. He sat very close to me and clung onto my arm throughout the session. He did open up to her and told her what he was scared about. He loved it that she had Grover [a Sesame Street character] in her office and she let him hold him. He talked about Grover during the week and on the way to his next visit.

The next time he opened up more. His therapist told him the story of Henny Penny. As she did that he started to rub his tummy and almost went to sleep on her ottoman. I remember she asked him how he felt when he rubbed his tummy like that. He said that that felt good, and he didn't feel so scared when he rubbed his tummy. She told him he could do that whenever he wanted to and he could tell himself how good it felt. He could do it every time he wanted to feel more comfortable.

By the time we came for our third interview, Timothy was doing much better. The therapist played a game with him. He stayed with her while I went just outside the door and came right back.

Then he went out into the passageway by himself. Then we repeated it, this time by my going down to the end of the hall. By then he was well on his way and gradually clung less and less.

Timothy is seven now. He quickly returned to his normal, easygoing self. In fact, I have to keep an eye on him! If ever we are separated in a store or such he doesn't panic at all. He visits friends and stays overnight without even mentioning us.

He's a very happy little boy again. He is still uncomfortable about death, and when his grandmother and grandfather's sister died this year, he prayed for each of these people. When he asked us, "Why does God take the people we love?" we did our best to explain about everyone having to die at some time. We also told him that everyone feels sad and sorrowful when people they love die. We think his reaction to death is pretty normal now.

When I told Timothy I was writing this story, he asked, "Does she still have Grover?"

Christine and Nichole's Story
(Told by their mother)

I brought the girls to see a therapist because I was concerned about the symptoms they were manifesting. Christine had started having lots of accidents, and Nichole was having horrible nightmares and frequent tummyaches. The symptoms started right after they had been to visit their father, who lives in another state.

Christine was just a year old and Nichole was two and a half when their father and I were first separated. The divorce took place a year after that, and we lived in the same town as the girls' father for another six months. During this time they visited him every other weekend during the daytime. On one of the times we had planned they would stay overnight, Nichole screamed so much he brought them back at around midnight.

Six months after we moved here I took the girls to be with their father for two weeks. I stayed nearby with my mother, and the girls called me often and came to visit me a couple of times. Each time, they did not want to return to their father. Their symptoms started as soon as we came home again.

I tried to be positive about their visits by telling the girls that their daddy wanted to see them very much and that because he could not see them very often he had all sorts of fun things planned to do with them. I also thought that being nearby and available on the telephone and for visits would be helpful to them.

After we returned home Nichole began having nightmares. I went into her room, soothed her, and tried to calm her down. With Christine's accidents, I made as little of them as possible. I reminded her about going to the bathroom more often during the day and made sure she did not drink close to bedtime. But the symptoms continued.

When I brought the girls to therapy, you encouraged them to bring their thoughts and feelings out into the open. That helped a great deal, especially with Nichole. Once it was out on the table and the problem behavior was identified, she became aware of what she was doing, and that put her in better control. She loved what you taught her about dealing with her nightmares. You told her that if she woke up remembering a scary dream, she could immediately imagine a whole lot of helpers coming to deal with and overpower whatever was scaring her. She loved that idea and practiced thinking of other ideas. The next time she had a nightmare she was ready with her army who demolished her monster in short order. She told me about it the next day and we giggled over it. Her nightmares stopped.

When the therapist talked to her about her tummyaches, she asked her what would be going on in there to make her feel so uncomfortable. She came up with the idea that it felt as if there were a whole bunch of little people in there jumping around and having a party. Then the therapist asked her to think about what would quiet them down. She decided she'd rub her tummy and tell them it was time to stop. She found she felt good when she did that.

You told me you thought the best thing to do for Christine's bed-wetting was a little hypnosis. You started to talk to Christine about when she was a tiny baby and all the things she knew how to do without knowing that she knew them. She knew how to keep herself breathing all day and all night without even thinking about it; she knew how to suck and swallow; and she knew how to keep her blood moving all around her body. Then, as she grew, she learned how to do all sorts of other things like walking and talking. She learned how to wait a little while when she felt like going to the bathroom. She may not have realized how she did that, but she did learn how to do it. She did it by tightening all those little muscles that stopped her having an accident. You told Christine to practice tightening them and letting them go right then. She did it and smiled broadly. Then you told Christine to practice that a lot that week. She could even practice it while she was going to the bathroom. She could practice starting and stopping as much as she wanted and she'd become very good at doing that whenever she needed to give herself time to get to the toilet. Finally, you told Christine you didn't think she'd have many more accidents if she had any at all, and very soon the problem would be over. It was.

Altogether we had five or six therapy sessions. I learned how important it is to talk about what bothers us, to identify problem behavior, and find solutions that work. I also became much more aware of how different the two girls are in the way they deal with their problems. Christine denies that she has any, but develops symptoms. Nichole exaggerates how terrible everything is and is verbal and expressive about her worries.

When children are between three and six, they are imaginative and scare themselves easily, they think magically, are likely to have nightmares, and they are highly suggestible. They are old enough to know there is a relationship between events and outcomes, but not old enough to distinguish between fantasy and reality. It is the prime time for anxiety problems to begin. All three children were anxious when they came.

One of the effective ways of helping children who are anxious is by using Eriksonian hypnosis. I was privileged to spend a week with Milton Erickson, M.D., just before he died. At age ninety, he was still considered the leading authority on medical hypnosis and loved to retell stories about people whose problems had been solved through hypnosis. The method I used, which is described in Christine's mother's story, is one I learned from him as he told of a young boy who'd had chronic problems with bed wetting. The story of Henny Penny I told Timothy was partly as I remembered it from my own childhood and partly what I made up as I went along with the hope and expectation that Timothy would apply the story to his undue concern. Here's an abbreviated version of my story:

One day as Henny Penny was eating her breakfast in the farm yard, a pea fell on her head. She was so frightened that she thought the sky was falling. She ran to Cocky Locky in a panic and told him to come with her to tell the King the sky was falling. As they ran they called out to tell all the other animals they saw, and they all joined the procession and ran as hard as they could. Then, as they saw a wise old owl—Owlly Wowly. The noise they were making awakened him from his sleep. Instead of joining the crowd, he said, "Wait a minute!! It will take weeks to get to the King's palace, and it's already quite dark. Show me where you were when you felt the sky falling." So they turned around and Henny Penny went back to the exact spot. The wise owl saw the pea, picked it up with his beak and dropped it again, right on Henny Penny's head. "There it is again," she said.

Timothy looked half asleep and stretched all over my ottoman by the time the farmyard procession was on its way. Almost as soon as I spoke about the Owl telling the processions to stop, he began to rub his tummy. He had already started to comfort himself. By the time the owl had dropped the pea, Timothy was murmuring "Mmm...Mmm."

The method I taught Nichole for dealing with her dreams is an adaptation of Senoi Dream work. The Senoi Indians live in Southeast Asia and meet together daily to work with their dreams. They teach young children to confront in fantasy the scary things in their dreams by providing them with allies stronger than the things that are scaring them in their dreams. After the confrontation and still with the allies present, the dreamers talk with whomever or whatever scared them and ask the scary thing to tell them what lesson they can learn from the dream. Then they thank their powerful allies for being available.

PART TWO

HOW THERAPY
WORKS

Section One

The Way We Work as Therapists

When people come to us for therapy, the first thing we want to know is why they have come and what they want to have happen as a result of their work with us. When this is clear, we then make a contract or agreement with them. A number of things are contained in this agreement that defines how we work and what their part in treatment is. We believe that "the power is in the patient," to quote one of our colleagues, and it is important to establish from the beginning that there are no fairy godmothers or magic wands. Results come in therapy by the people setting well defined goals and working hard to achieve those goals. The therapist is a kind of midwife to help the client achieve his (her) objectives.

While we are finding out a client's goals and objectives, we are making our initial decision about how best to work with this client. Will he (she) get on best in individual, couple, or group therapy? Rather quickly we need to make another decision. Is this person asking for symptom relief? Or is he (she) asking for self-understanding at a deeper and more internal level, which means working at just below the surface level of consciousness? Or is this a person who wants to delve even deeper into his (her) psyche and deal with the unconscious? We have an initial perception of the level at which the client seems to want to work, but we are always open to working on another level if that is chosen once the client understands conceptually what is involved in working at each level.

If a certain client wants only symptom relief, this is usually accomplished in a few sessions. There we discuss the problem he (she) faces, talk about options for solving it, how he (she) will experiment with and choose the most likely of these options, and how to evaluate the outcomes of the choice. You may want to look at the section on "problem solving" techniques, page 137, to understand better how you can use this approach.

If a person has chosen to work at level two—that of deeper self-understanding and of becoming aware of his (her) internal dialogue—then we use the material described in our book *Aging With Joy* (Twenty-Third Publications), Chapter Six, "Talking to Yourself Is OK."

Many people feel satisfied to have symptom relief or to gain more understanding about how they talk to themselves inside their own heads, and how this affects the way they feel and behave. Many others find that this is not enough. For them, an understanding of their unconscious is essential. We have four ways of working with unconscious material. The first is what we call "little work." The purpose of it is to meet unmet early childhood needs. In Part Two we describe how and why we work with this method. Our second way of working with unconscious material is called "Re-decision Work." In this process, a person is guided to relive early traumatic experiences which are at the root of the present problem.

All children suffer painful childhood experiences, and all children carry with them the memory and wounding of those experiences. For some people the damage is severe enough to be of tremendous harm to their development, achievement, and happiness. If this is so, then we find that a reliving of the early scene or scenes provides an opportunity for healing. When a person is willing to re-experience and relive early pain, the therapist acts as protective Parent to their inner Child. With that protection, the Child is given permission to be his (her) honest self and redo the traumatic scene substituting another and happier ending. This is what we call "getting a new show on the road." We believe that Life is on the side of health and wholeness, so that the courageous experience of reliving earlier pain and being willing to make a happier ending is similar to a surgical lancing of a boil. The infection is drained and healthy tissue begins to bring healing from deep inside the wounded psyche.

We believe that the major and magical decisions of a person's life are made by the time that person is six years old. Major decisions are made at a conscious level and then put out of awareness by young children and are based on information children have gathered from their world. The most significant parts of a child's world are his experiences with his parents or his caretakers. If these "big" people are damaged in their psyches, they will give the child incorrect information. The child will not know this is incorrect and will build his life as if what he has been told and what he has seen modeled is indeed true. He will live with these "truths" for the rest of his life unless he runs into trouble and has a chance to make new decisions based on his own life experience rather than on archaic information from his childhood.

In many of the stories our clients have written, they referred to their own experiences of "re-decision" and "little work" that have come as a result of what they learned by reliving some of the pain of their childhood. If you are especially interested in how these methods work, you will want to reread their stories.

In addition to "little work" and "redecision therapy," we have a third way of working with unconscious material. This is "dream analysis" and here we are indebted to Dr. Carl Jung who believed that our unconscious self speaks to our conscious self through the language of dreams. Dr. Sigmund Freud once said that "Dreams are the royal road to the unconscious." Jung made dream analysis the major part of his psychoanalytic method. Unlike Freud, Jung believed not only in the personal unconscious, but also posited a collective unconscious common to all humankind. Our personal and our collective unconscious are the home not only of the dark side of ourselves but also and equally the home of the angels. For those who want to explore the full depth of themselves, working with dreams holds the promise of discovering the shadow and the fullness of the spiritual and mystical aspects of the psyche. The symbols and images of our dreams yield the richness of the depth of our souls, and Jung believed that in working with those symbols and images, we grow in awareness of our own worth and our potential for beauty and wholeness.

For readers who may want to explore the world of dreams and dream analysis, we suggest the following reading: 1) Jung's autobiography, *Memories, Dreams and Reflections,* 2) Jung's *Man and His Symbols,* 3) Robert Johnson's *Inner Work.*

Our fourth way of working with unconscious material is through hypnosis. Unlike many therapists who use hypnosis, we do not hypnotize adults. This is in keeping with our belief that adults need to take charge of their own therapy and that we are there to help them accomplish their goals, not do for them what they are able to do for themselves. We therefore teach adults how to do self-hypnosis. We do hypnotize children when it is clear that this procedure is called for.

We think of hypnosis as an altered state of consciousness much the same as sleep or deep meditation, when we allow our conscious and unconscious minds to touch and communicate with each other. Hypnosis is a powerful and effective tool for such purposes as changing destructive habits, controlling or curing pain, and helping a person to recall repressed material from the unconscious which can only be dealt with when it is brought into consciousness.

When we teach adults how to hypnotize themselves, we also teach them how to develop their own program to use while they are in hypnosis. In this way they are in charge of their own program for their behavior and habit control or for their own pain relief while they are in a hypnotized state. Many of these people use their acquired pain control skill when they go to the dentist. Others use it to reduce pain from arthritis, bursitis, chronic headaches, etc.

In this discussion of how we work, it should be clear to the reader that many times it is important for the person coming into therapy to begin to understand his or her own childhood experiences. All adults have at one time been children, but many of us have never had the opportunity to know what healthy and unhealthy child development is. Many of us have only our own experience to go by and we may easily conclude that our childhood was natural to all childhood experience. In the next section we will talk about what we see as the early stages of child development.

Section Two

Early Childhood Development

In the last section, we indicated that there are various levels of the human psyche, and that the person coming for counsel and the therapist decide together at which level it is best to begin. Whenever a person comes to deal with long-standing issues or an understanding of his (her) unconscious, it is essential sooner or later that that person begin to understand his (her) early development. Of course, much took place that need not be looked at, but whatever early experiences affect a person today do need to be understood so that the healing of childhood suffering and pain can take place.

This section will deal with child development in sufficient degree to give you our understanding of how children develop from the time they are born until they are six years old. This section provides insight into the stories in Part One.

At birth, all but severely handicapped infants have the potential to grow and develop to maturity and autonomy. Each child has the potential to become either a well-adjusted, productive, and joyful person or a troubled, irresponsible, or dissatisfied human being. What makes the difference?

For generations, theoreticians have argued and researched: Is it heredity or environment? More recently some theoreticians have been asking, is it early childhood experience or biological make-

up? Others have been researching parenting styles and birth order differences. Our belief is that the ease with which children develop is not determined by any one factor alone, but rather by five
important factors.

1. The nature of the child. Children are not all alike when they
are born. Some are active, others relaxed; some noisy, others
quiet; some have healthy appetites, others have to be coaxed to
eat; some fight going to sleep so they'll not miss a thing, while
others love to sleep. Each of these characteristics will have an effect upon the way the child learns and the way others nurture and
respond to his (her) needs.

2. The personalities of parents, other significant caretakers, and
siblings. Caretakers who love having children around will influence them quite differently from those who resent their presence.

3. The birth order of the child. Being the oldest child, the
youngest, the only girl among several boys, or the only boy
among girls makes a difference in the expectations of not only
parents but also of siblings.

4. The nature of the relationship that develops between the
child and the significant people in his early years. The way parents and siblings nurture children and interact with them, as well
as the way different children respond, are both significant in de-
termining the type of relationship that will develop. This may be
cooperative, competitive, loving, or hostile. Whatever the result, it
will have important effects upon how comfortable children feel
about themselves and others.

5. The decisions the child makes about life by the time he (she)
is six years old. Children make important decisions such as:

"I'm smart" or "I'm dumb."
"It's good I'm here" or "I'm in the way."
"I'm important" or "I'm not important."
"It's OK to ask" or "I mustn't ask."
"Other people are OK" or "Other people are not OK"
"Men are kind, mean, jolly, or absent."
"Women are loving, frazzled, fun, or sick."
"I can trust others" or "I can't trust."

Children reach these conclusions based on their early experience. Then they act as if the conclusions are true in all sorts of situations.

Children have needs from the moment of birth. The parents' job is to rear the child by providing for these needs until he (she) reaches adulthood. Initially this involves a relationship where the child is completely dependent and the parents are totally responsible for providing for the child's needs. Once the fully dependent relationship has been formed it needs to be followed by a step-by-step resolution of the dependency so that the child will develop abilities to move through a stage of independence to autonomy and maturity.

At each stage of development children have specific sets of needs. As these needs are met they are ready and happy to move onto the next stage. When needs are not met satisfactorily children will either resist going to the next stage or over-adapt in one of many ways to be explained as we go along.

Each stage of a child's development is important, and none is more important than the first one because each stage builds the foundation for the next.

Stage 1

From Birth to Crawling: Up to About Nine Months

Children come into the world with many innate abilities. They are in touch with their needs and they have no hesitation about letting others know when they are uncomfortable in any way. They know how to ask and they know when they have had enough. When parents anticipate their child's every need so that the child never has to ask for anything, they deny the child the opportunity to learn that he (she) can do something to communicate and solve problems.

Children learn to adapt their behavior and reach conclusions about themselves very early. When people respond consistently to their cries they learn, "I can ask," "It's all right for me to have needs," "I get my needs met when I ask," When people do not respond or respond inconsistently, infants become confused and may conclude, "I'm not supposed to ask," or "My needs don't matter." Similarly, infants can tell by the way they are picked up, held, and fed whether or not people are glad they are here, and will conclude, "I'm loved and wanted" or "I'm in the way." Consistent responses also communicate "You can depend on me," "You can trust me," and "I'll take care of you."

Newborn children need to experience safe limits. One of the biggest transitions a newborn child has to make is suddenly being thrust into a situation which no longer provides the familiar and safe confined limits of the womb. Babies need to be held close, cuddled, rocked, and tucked in firmly. They also need to be put down so they can learn that they are separate from others. Being put down enables them to learn where they finish, that they are with themselves all the time and other people come and go.

By the time children can sit up they have their first impressions about whether they are loved, wanted, real, separate, safe, and whether it is OK to have needs and to ask to have them met. They will also know who belongs in their house and who is a stranger. Most will go through a stage where they do not welcome strangers and certainly do not want them to minister to their needs.

Stage 2

From Crawling to Running: Nine to 18 Months

Learning to crawl enables children to be mobile and to experience the first taste of autonomy. Now they can choose whether or not they will crawl across the room to get a goodie. Very soon they will begin to explore every nook and cranny within their reach.

Having the freedom (within safe limits) to explore, to open and empty cupboards, and make noises with things provides children with important learning opportunities. They find that learning can be fun, that they can control some things, and that there is a relationship between what they do and the result, e.g., banging lids makes a noise.

As soon as they can walk with ease, they feel more mobile, taller, and powerful. They learn new tricks daily and know what to do to get themselves in the midst of whatever goes on around them. They delight in showing other people how smart they are. It is important for them to be affirmed with positive strokes for the things they can do. It is even more important that they continue to get a healthy supply of positive, unconditional strokes. They also need sufficient negative conditional strokes to keep them safe (see p. 134).

Ideally, by the end of this period, children know that they are loved, wanted, and liked for who they are; that they can learn and do things, and ask for what they want and need. They will also feel safe and know they can depend on their caretakers.

Stage 3

From Saying "No" to Saying "Yes," "No," or "Maybe": Eighteen Months to Three Years

This is a period of testing and one which many parents find difficult. The major questions children put to the test during this time are: Who is in charge here? Will you still love me if I say no to you? Will you still be there if I run away from you?

The first question is the one which many parents find most difficult. It is important that parents let these little ones know that they (the parents) are in charge. Although all two year olds want to think they are the boss, they need to learn they are not. Two year olds are just not old enough to know what is good or safe for them to do. They have no capacity to take care of themselves or their needs. They do need to be listened to, to know it is all right for them to ask for what they want to realize that sometimes the answer is no. We advise that whenever a child of this age is told "No, you can't do (have) that," there be at least two things the child can do or have, e.g., "No, you cannot play with the knife. You can have your bear or this apple."

Children need to be dealt with consistently, firmly, and gently. When parents give in to children after a temper tantrum, children learn that having tantrums pays off and so they'll be likely to have many more. The sooner children learn that their parents are in charge, the easier it is for them and everyone else. Children of this age feel insecure and unprotected when it is not clear to them that a big person is responsible and in control.

The second question, "Will you still love me if I say no to you?" presents much less of a problem in the minds of most parents, however, many children become confused about this when they sense rejection after having been difficult. This is the reason why it is important to communicate to children over and over that they are loved and liked. Sometimes their behavior is not acceptable and needs to be changed, but they never need negative unconditional strokes. (See page 134.)

The third question, "Will you still be there if I run away from you?" is one which most children answer for themselves. At some point children will want to get out of sight. At this stage they will usually not go very far before they get scared and peep around the corner to ensure that someone is still there. By the end of this period children will feel most comfortable knowing parents are in charge and are still available when they test limits.

Stage 4

From Nursery to School Child: Three to Six Years

At this stage children have a consuming curiosity. They are high-ly intuitive, learn quickly, have vivid imaginations, and do not distinguish between magic and reality. During this time they come to the realization that boys and girls are different and are intrigued with the difference. They come to know that boys grow into men and girls into women and they develop attachments to their parent of the opposite sex. Toward the end of this period they will be in kindergarten or school and will be learning about making their own friends separate from their families.

In addition to continuing to be affirmed, children in this stage need some new encouragements and permissions. They benefit from exposure to a variety of situations and from people who are willing to answer endless questions. It is important for them to learn that, while it is all right to be cute, they don't need to be cute in order to be loved. They need permission and encouragement to have and express their ideas and to be close to both parents.

This is the age when children frequently hear much about being good and bad. Because they think magically, they often make up and believe things that haunt them in later life. For example, Al was often jealous of his little sister. When he was four, she was killed in an accident. He decided it was his fault. He did not talk to anyone about it for fear of punishment, but he lived with the assumption until he dealt with it in therapy years later. Parents cannot protect their children from their own magical conclusions. Whenever there are tragedies in families who have children of this age, however, it is wise to reassure them that they did not make the tragedy happen. Once again, it is important for children to learn to distinguish between doing something that is wrong and being a bad person.

During most of this period children still think magically. They are highly intuitive, have vivid imaginations, and make decisions about themselves and others which they carry into adulthood. Once these decisions are made children live with them as though they were facts. For example, a child may decide, "The only way I can stay out of trouble is to keep my thoughts to myself." From that time on he becomes more and more hesitant to express himself. When he does say what he thinks he is likely to do so in such a way that he will invite criticism and this criticism will confirm his earlier decision.

Children also learn that when they express some feelings they get what they want and when they express other feelings they are punished or ignored. In some families, for example, it is not OK to be angry, while in others anger is encouraged. When a child is punished for feeling angry but is given attention for being sad, he is likely to learn how to act sad whenever he is angry as well as when he is sad. Another child may be ignored if he acts sad but given attention when he begins to be anxious or agitated. Then he is likely to become chronically anxious and agitated. The feelings which cover over real feelings are often called "racket feelings."

These four stages encompass the years that we believe are the most important in the child's psychological development. By the time children are six they have reached decisions about themselves, discovered which feelings are most likely to elicit a nonthreatening response from others, and how to behave in ways that will confirm their assumptions. Problems that show up in later years can almost always be shown to have their initial beginning in this birth-to-six-year-old period.

Section Three

Little Work—Re-Parenting

The process of maintaining emotional and psychological well-being is much like taking good care of a house. We all know that many little things and some big things can and do go wrong from time to time. Depending on the nature of the problem, we can determine whether we can fix it ourselves, ask a friend or family member to help, or need to call in a professional. Similarly, we have the choice of fixing it right away, putting it on a list of things to be done later, or ignoring it altogether.

Preventive care, doing cosmetic work, and dealing with little problems as they occur reduces the risk of major problems arising. However, even with care, houses without firm foundations will cause endless and sometimes dramatic problems until someone digs down and rebuilds them in a satisfactory way. Similarly, when people feel as if their psychological foundations are falling out from under them and their old coping mechanisms are not working, intervention becomes a necessity.

In the previous section, we outlined the most important needs to be met if children are to have a firm foundation for life. When these needs are not met, children will not only overadapt by becoming too anxious to please, stubborn, rebellious, helpless, over-achieving, or withdrawn, but also continue to grow with faulty foundations. Mostly, they will hurt inside and think there's something wrong with them, but they will not know what it is. Often, like Ann, Connie, and Dana—whose stories you read earlier— they will go to extremes to hide their pain from others. Sometimes, like Krys and Sara, they will become dramatic in their cries for help.

It is very sad when people suffer for years because their needs have never been met and they have reached all sorts of false conclusions about themselves and the world. However, there is something that can be done. Early childhood needs which have not been met before can be met now. That is what "little work" or "reparenting" is all about. What we do in "little work" is to identify what needs have not been met, identify the age when they could have been met, and then plan to meet them now.

We explain the situation with the person concerned. If the person is willing to do "little work," we set up a clearly defined contract as to how this will be done. Sometimes this may be for a few minutes. Occasionally, at other times, it may be for extended periods. The story which follows will illustrate how we do this.

Rosie was referred by her probation officer. She'd been charged with lewd and disruptive behavior after having been caught running around nude on a busy street. She'd been on probation once before, had been diagnosed as manic-depressive, and had had Lithium prescribed for her. Once on Lithium, she had stopped acting out, finished the final semester of her degree, and found a job. Everyone who knew her had thought she was a "different person."

The problem that Rosie had had with this was that she didn't want to be a "different person." She wanted to be the Rosie she knew, and so she had decided Lithium was her enemy and stopped taking it. She had begun going to work when she felt like it, had argued with her boss, and had been fired. She broke off with her boyfriend, went on spending sprees, and got a speeding ticket before her indecent behavior charge. Now, she said she was depressed because all she had were bills, bills, bills and a probation officer—none of which she wanted. She could not believe she had been so crazy.

I asked her, "What's in it for you to act so crazy?" She looked at me and her eyes sparkled, "Ha, ha,...*excitement!* Life is so dull when I take that Lithium. Why should I settle for that? I'm damned if I do and I'm damned if I don't. All I can do is be bored to death or finish up in prison, but I'd kill myself before I'd go to prison."

Rosie's problems went back to when she was very little. Her most vivid memories were of being yelled at by her parents for being such a hellion, for doing such things as leaving the house at night and hiding where no one could find her, climbing onto the roof, and on one occasion setting fire to some grass near their house. She also remembered being compared with her older sister, who was the good and responsible one; her younger brother, who was the smart one; and her little sister, who was everybody's darling and so much younger that nothing was expected of her.

She had never been provided with consistent and safe limits. She had no memory of ever having been told things like, "Stop doing that!" or "You are not to go outside at night." Instead she was told how bad she was for doing dangerous things, and she felt very powerful because she could get such a lot of adult energy invested in her. She also had no memories of her parents doing things with her that were fun or telling her what she could do that would be exciting and yet safe.

I told Rosie I'd be willing to work with her for her ten authorized sessions on condition that she take her Lithium as prescribed and that she make a "no suicide" contract. She was willing to do those two things, and we developed a treatment contract whereby she would learn to set safe limits for herself and find safe and harmless ways to have fun and excitement in her life. Ten weeks was not a long time for psychotherapy for someone who was manic-depressive, but it was long enough to do something significant.

The best time for children to start learning that they can do things that are fun and yet safe is when they are at the exploratory stage of their development—at about twelve to fifteen months of age. We structured her therapy sessions as follows:

1. The first ten minutes or so Rosie reported in about the previous week. I encouraged and affirmed her for anything she had

done to take good care of herself—looking for a job, finding a job, going out with friends, etc. Whenever she reported something good that had happened, I had her identify what she had done to help bring that about.

2. Next, Rosie did "little work" for about 15–20 minutes. During this time she became a twelve-month-old child, and I became her parent for that time. She could do all the things children of that age can do. She walked, crawled, scooted, picked up everything in sight, put things in her mouth, attempted to climb on the furniture. She played with some of the toys and ignored others, sat and went to sleep in my lap, and screamed when I would not let her go near the lamps or other places where she could hurt herself. She tested me over and over again with things she knew I would not let her do, such as climbing onto the window sill. She learned that if I said "Stop that" I meant it, and if she continued I'd do something to better "baby proof" the room. She also learned that I noticed her for doing ordinary things and that she did not have to be provocative to get my attention.

3. When it was time, I'd tell her to grow up. Then we'd discuss what she had experienced that day—how she felt and what she had learned. As she became comfortable at each age level we decided how old she would be the following week.

4. The final part of the session was spent planning ways to have a good week. During her last session we spent the whole time planning how she could live a constructive life. I referred her to another therapist who lives where she planned to move to as soon as her probation was over.

PART THREE

CHANGING YOUR LIFE

Section One

How You Can Help Yourself

You too can begin to change your life, just as the people who have written their stories in this book were able to make changes in their lives. They have related their experiences with us and told us how therapy helped them. Whether or not therapy is needed for making changes depends on the problems a person wants to solve. Some things, such as phobias or script re-decision, need a therapist's help. In other instances, we need a third person to help us see our blind spots. Some people who have had serious deprivation in their early years need "little work" and" re-parenting."

If you are thinking of going to a therapist, here are some guidelines we think will be of help to you:

1. Find a therapist who is recommended by two people.
2. Check out cost, insurances, method of payment, length of sessions, cancellation policy, and the expected time for fulfilling your needs.
3. Look for a therapist who is well qualified, understanding, and concerned. You should have a good rapport with the person you choose.
4. Make a second appointment only if you begin to feel better after the first appointment. If not, find someone else.

5. Do not continue with a therapist who wants to hospitalize you at your first appointment unless you are highly suicidal, homicidal, chemically addicted, or losing touch with reality.

In our book *Aging with Joy*, we devote an entire chapter to this subject of professional help. You may want to read the chapter if you are interested in knowing more about this subject. In this present section, however, we want to discuss things you can do to make changes in yourself without the help of psychotherapy. Our first suggestion is that you read a book by Muriel James and Dorothy Joungward, *Born to Win*. This is an excellent introduction to Transactional Analysis (T.A.), a system of psychological understanding begun about thirty years ago by a California psychiatrist, Dr. Eric Berne. His theories and ways of working as a therapist were so potent that many other psychiatrists, social workers, psychologists, and counselors expanded and developed Dr. Berne's original work. In several life stories in this book, people told how much they were helped by understanding this system. *Born to Win* is an inexpensive paperback and will give you a lot of practical help as you seek to make changes in your life.

In the following pages we outline some things that can help you as you exchange worry for wellness. We are indebted to several of our colleagues for some of the material that follows. Dr. Eric Berne for his original work on ego states, wherein he divides the ego into three parts (Parent, Adult, Child); Dr. Berne again for the material on strokes; Jacqui Schiff, M.S.W., for the material on "Passivity" and on "Discounting;" Taibi Kahler, Ph.D., for "Drivers and Allowers;" Dr. Steven Karpman for "The Drama Triangle;" and Dr. Robert and Mary Goulding for material on "Injunctions." We have adapted some of their material for our use in this book, and we hope that you will find it useful.

Ego States

Eric Berne, M.D. observed that each person functions in three different and distinctive ways: Parent, Adult, and Child. He called these ego states and diagrammed them as on page 132.

He observed that when a person is functioning in one of his ego states and then changes to another, he is like a different person. As an example, a person who sits still and quietly discusses and develops serious plans in a matter of fact way with his wife at one moment, may suddenly yell, throw his arms around, jump up and down, and have a sudden burst of energy when the ball game comes on the television. It is as if he has instantly changed from being an adult and become an eight-year-old child again. If the

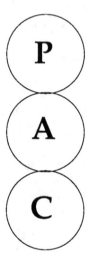

telephone rings and he learns there's an emergency and a friend is in need he may suddenly change again. This time he immediately moves from being like a young child to being a responsible, caring, and involved person who relates to his friend as a parent does to his children.

The job of the Parent is to
   have values
   make judgments
   care for self and others
   protect self and others from harm
   set limits

The Parent has two functions: critical and nurturing. Both critical and nurturing functions may operate in constructive or destructive ways. Some examples of Parent statements are:

"Don't lie!"	Constructive Critical Parent
"You're dumb!"	Descriptive Critical Parent
"Well done!"	Constructive Nurturing Parent
"Don't bother to do your work."	Destructive Nurturing Parent

The job of the Adult is to
    collect information
    store information
    recall information
    reason
    analyze facts and figures.

Some examples of Adult statements are:
    "There are twenty chairs here."
    "I went to school in Boston."
    "Summer temperatures are hotter than winter ones."

The job of the Child is to
    feel and express feelings
    have needs and wants
    sense
    intuit
    eat, drink, and have fun.

The Child has two functions: natural and adapted. Both natural and adapted functions may act in appropriate or inappropriate ways, depending on the situation. Some examples are as follows:

Natural Child	"Let's have fun!"
	"That feels good."
	"Yuk!"
	"I want what I want when I want it."

Adapted Child   "I'm scared at parties."
                             "I'll wait until you're ready."
                             "Please pass the butter."

People who are healthy psychologically can move from one ego
state to another quickly as the situation warrants.

Strokes

Unlike a physical stroke which is damaging and sometimes fatal,
a stroke, as we use the word, is something very positive, indeed
essential for emotional health. The term was first used by those in
Transactional Analysis (T.A.) to mean any recognition which is
given by one person to another.

In practice there are four types of strokes: 1) positive conditional, 2) negative conditional, 3) positive unconditional, and 4) negative unconditional. A positive conditional stroke is given with a
condition attached; for example, "I like you *because* you get good
grades, are a good employee, a dutiful wife, a good basketball
player, funny," etc.

The negative conditional stroke also has a condition attached;
for example, "You're a bad boy *because* you didn't cut the lawn...
You flunked geometry... You didn't come in on time," etc.   The
positive unconditional stroke is given just for being you, with no
condition attached: "I love you...It's great to have you here...
You're my honey," etc.

The negative unconditional also has no condition attached:
"You're a bad girl...Get away...You're awful," etc.

We know that newborns want and need positive unconditional
stroking, and we also know that all of us thrive and glow with
this kind of stroking. We all want to be appreciated, wanted, and
loved. If these positive unconditional strokes are never or almost
never given, the child, and later the grown-up will then look next
for positive conditional strokes, that is, approval for achievements, personality, appearance, possessions, etc.: "Like me for
what I can do or for what I have."

If a person does not get sufficient recognition and stroking in either of these two ways, he will then try for negative conditional stroking: "By making mistakes, messing up, and getting into trouble, at least I get noticed." This may seem like strange behavior, but we are so linked together in human community that we are even willing to get into trouble in order to get noticed. The last kind of stroking, unconditional negative, is a desperate attempt to have some kind of attention. We do see people who stay, tragically, with others who abuse and misuse them: husbands with wives, wives with husbands, employees with employers, friends with friends. Abused children have no place to go. Most grownups do have choices, and when they stay in situations in which they are abused, the pattern of negative unconditional stroking is all they believe they deserve.

A great deal of work in therapy is with people who want to change their stroking patterns in order to feel better about themselves and have more joy in living. No one deserves unconditional negative stroking. No one deserves only negative conditional stroking, either, although negative conditional strokes are part of adequate parenting and essential for the growth of all children (and adults) who act like undisciplined children. Everyone deserves positive stroking. Much positive conditional stroking is healthy and contributes to our sense of well-being and appreciation. But all of us need and deserve positive and unconditional strokes—lots of them.

You can learn to change your stroking pattern by being with people who like you just for yourself and will not dump their own bad tempers and moods on you. You can learn to stroke yourself by becoming a good Parent to your own inner Child. Remember, your emotional well-being depends on having a good stroke bank. Deposits can be made by other people and deposits can be made by you. You deserve the best!

Shrinking the Witch and Ogre
(The Ugly Voices in Your Head)

1. Imagine the witch or ogre to be nine feet tall. Then gradually

shrink her (him) a few inches. Keep doing this until you get her (him) down to a few inches. Now decide how to get rid of the witch or ogre and silence the ugly voice in your head.

2. Tell the witch or ogre to do whatever bad thing(s) they are telling you to do. Then act your way. Here are some examples:

    a. "You should work all the time."

      "I'll work, and I'll also play."

    b. "You should save more money."

      "I've saved enough. Now I'm going to spend some on a vacation."

    c. "You should clean up your house."

      "It's clean enough for me."

3. Poison Strokes:

When you hear voices in your head, or hear other people say things such as "You're stupid, slow, childish, too much trouble, not as good as..." etc., then you know you're being poisoned. Shut this message off.

Now, put in a message of healing and wholeness, such as: "I'm intelligent enough to do what I need to do. I'm not childish; I have a fun child within me that likes to play. I don't need to compare myself with others. I'm me and glad of it."

Freeing the Child

1. Fun List: List all the things which are fun for you and which are possible to do at this time in your life. Then, make a contract with yourself that you will do at least one of these things each day. Here are some ideas from fun lists we have seen: Walk barefoot, lick an ice cream cone, get a hug, take a hot bath, get a back rub, walk, bike, etc.

2. Caring Parent Messages: List all the things you would like to hear from a loving caretaker. Select at least one each day and say it to your little Child. (Put a pillow or doll on your lap and let it represent your little Child, then talk to it.) Ideas: "I love you. I'm glad you're you. You're fun. I like being with you." etc.

3. Friends: Pick someone you like and agree to exchange fun,

problems, and joys at least once a week.

4. Funny faces: Make faces in the mirror, then later get a friend to make funny faces with you.

5. Get noticed: Ask for what you want. Come on time if you're always late. Speak up if you're usually quiet.

6. Play act: Imagine what you would have done if you hadn't become the person you are. Then imagine the clothes you'd wear, how you'd walk, speak, act.

Problem-Solving Techniques

If you have a problem that needs solving, activate your Adult by following specific steps: Some steps may not apply to all problems, but at least consider them as you move through the process.

1. What does the Parent in your head say (shoulds, oughts, etc.)? How does your Child feel? What Adult information do you have?

2. What attitudes, feelings, and adaptations hinder problem solving?

3. What attitudes, feelings, and adaptations are helpful?

4. List 3 or 4 options for solving your problems. Play each one out in your head (...and then...and then...and then) and see how each comes out.

5. What resources, strengths do you have for problem solving?

6. Choose the option that seems best to you (OK with your caring Parent, good for your Child, appropriate to the situation, caring of others).

7. Implement your decision—test in a small way first if possible (trial balloon).

8. Evaluate: Make necessary adjustments or choose another option if needed.

The Drama Triangle
(How to Keep Yourself Miserable in Three Moves)

If you are frequently in trouble with other people or in imaginary trouble inside your head as you think about relationships with others, chances are that you are in The Drama Triangle. Dr. Steven Karpman, a California psychiatrist, believed that troubled relationships come from our relating out of positions we learned early in life as a way of keeping excitement in our lives; thus the idea of drama. Each position in the triangle will, given enough time, move us into one of the other positions, and finally the third. The positions are "Victim," "Persecutor," and "Rescuer."

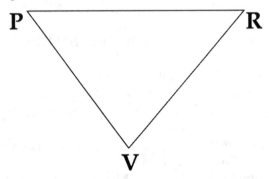

A "Victim" is not a true sufferer, but a person who thinks his trouble is caused entirely by other people. He operates out of a helpless position so that someone else will take responsibility for his suffering and will thereby "Rescue" him. Instead of looking for a "Rescuer," the "Victim" may look for a "Persecutor" who will criticize and "kick" him, thereby confirming the "Victim's" childhood decision that he is not OK.

A "Rescuer" is not someone who helps another in true need, but someone who plays big "Mommy" or "Daddy" by doing for another what the person is well able to do for himself. The "Rescuer" is unwilling to ask for what he/she wants, and secretly hopes to be loved by taking care of other people. When this doesn't happen, the "Rescuer" moves into "Persecutor" by saying, "After all I've done for you...."

A "Persecutor" may not be genuinely harming others, but may be the name given by the "Victim" to anyone who won't "dance to his tune"—a kind of perpetual two-year-old temper tantrum.

All three positions end in bad feelings for all the players in the drama. The only way out of the triangle is to refuse to play any of the parts. People who refuse to play in the drama take responsibility for their own lives and have straightforward, non-gamey relationships with other people. Note in Part One:

"Victim" stories (Sara, etc.)

"Rescuer" stories (Megan, Jean, Ann, etc.)

"Persecutor" stories (Maggie, Connie, etc. They thought other people were the cause of their troubles.)

Injunctions

When you were a child, your first learning came from what you saw, felt, and intuited. If you were cared for with tenderness, you learned that you were wanted and loved. If people around you were happy and enjoying each other, you learned that life was OK. When you began to understand words, if people set limits to protect you and yet gave you freedom to find your own way, you gradually discovered your own personality, learned from your mistakes, developed fairly normally and now have happy memories of your childhood.

If, on the other hand, you were born to parents who were already hurt themselves, and were unable to care for you, you probably thought you were not OK and that life was a burden. Wounded parents and caretakers give little children directions for living which hurt the growing process. First non-verbally, and then with words, they take away some of a child's birthright. As surely as malnutrition, physical abuse, and neglect damage a child's body, destructive messages damage a child's psyche.

Destructive non-verbal messages and a child's interpretation of them have been called "injunctions" because they live in the child's mind as prohibitions and commandments. A parent who is insecure and must therefore be overly domineering and bossy may be giving a child a "Don't think" injunction so that when the child develops he (she) may not use his (her) own thinking ability, but always wait to be commanded by others. In adult life this person will appear helpless and unable to make decisions. A parent who is afraid to show feelings may be saying to his (her) child, "Don't feel" or perhaps "Don't show your feelings." The little child then pushes away his (her) natural feelings, is ashamed of its anger, fear, or sadness, and grows up to be cold and insensitive to other people.

Some injunctions (strong messages damaging to wholeness) are:

1. "Don't be a child."
2. "Don't grow up."
3. "Don't think."
4. "Don't feel."
5. "Don't show your feelings."
6. "Don't succeed."
7. "Don't be the way you are."
8. "Don't be the sex you are."
9. "Don't be."

These injunctions from our earliest childhood continue as commandments for the rest of our lives unless we decide to divest them of their power. They can be changed. If you have one or more of them in your life pattern, it is important to stop believing it (them) and start living with healthy messages.

Discounting
(How to Stay Stuck)

It's always fun to find a bargain, to buy at discount, and save money. Discounting has another meaning, however, one that isn't fun if we do it or it's done to us. To discount may mean to cheapen or devaluate something that is of real value. Many people discount themselves, other people, and situations. One counselor, Jacqui Schiff, lists four ways we discount ourselves and our problems and thereby don't solve those problems. See if you do any of these.

1. Discount the problem itself by saying "I don't have a problem."

2. Discount the seriousness of the problem. "I'm depressed, but it doesn't matter."

3. Discount the solubility of the problem. "I have a problem and it's important, but no one can solve it."

4. Discount our ability to solve the problem. "I have a problem and it's important and maybe someone could solve it, but I can't."

Discounting in any of these ways keeps us stuck and suffering. The way to get on with wellness is to stop discounting and start doing what we need to do to solve our problem(s).

Passivity
(Non-Problem-Solving Behavior)

Children are naturally active and eager for life, but they quickly learn to hold back if they are not encouraged in their zest for new experiences. If they learn that they get into trouble with their caretakers when they make noise, crawl, explore, or investigate, they will soon withdraw and become passive, or they will become over-rebellious. They will also do the same thing if their caretakers are overly bossy. Domineering adults send this message to children: "I'll do your thinking for you and I'll make decisions for you. Your job is to do as you're told." The third cause of children becoming inert or over-rebellious comes when they see that if they do not take responsibility for their actions someone else will take it for them—a good way to avoid scoldings and punishment.

When we see passive children, adolescents, or adults, we know that either they have been frightened into that passivity by harsh treatment or they have chosen passivity as a way of getting out of responsibility. Someone else will take it for them. Passivity may be protective, but the price of protecting oneself in this way is everlasting immaturity. Here is the way passivity works. I have a problem—then:

1. I decide to do nothing to solve that problem.

2. I then cover over my true feelings of sadness, fear, or anger that are connected to my problem. This cover-up is done to please

someone who, I believe, is more powerful than I am. By pretending, I hope to stay out of trouble with this person.

3. Since adaptive behavior is "phony" and not honest, I become uncomfortable with myself and I begin to agitate, that is, I begin to do things that do not solve my problems. Examples of agitation are biting my nails, swinging my foot, crying hysterically, screaming, eating too much or too little, smoking, and drinking too much.

4. Agitation does nothing to solve my problem, and so out of prolonged frustration, I will then become either incapacitated or violent.

People who have learned passivity as a way of handling stress can unlearn passive behaviors and find more effective ways to solve their problems.

Dealing with Unpleasant Feelings

Feelings of anger, fear, and sadness are human, as well as universally experienced and expressed by all children by the time they are a few months old.

Anger results in an immediate involuntary supply of adrenaline which floods our bodies and gives us a burst of energy. Fear's immediate response is shock and stiffness, followed by a surplus of adrenaline. Sadness reduces energy.

When feelings are repressed or ignored, they do not leave but rather stay in our bodies, blocking the normal flow of energy and thus leading to physical pain or to anxiety, depression, resentment, and the like. When feelings are expressed, however, they go away and we can return to comfortable living.

We need to find effective ways of giving expression to feelings, ways that are safe and do not hurt ourselves, others, or the environment. We develop these ideas more fully beginning on page 144.

Drivers and Allowers

Many people feel as if they have a powerful force in them which seems to drive them instead of their being in charge of their behavior. These forces were first identified and given names by Dr. Taibi Kahler. The key idea to whether you are propelled by one or more of the drivers is its repetitive nature.

The five ways we drive ourselves are by listening to these imperatives:

1. "Hurry up."
2. "Please me."
3. "Be strong."
4. "Try hard."
5. "Be perfect."

Such drivers can be divested of their power to run our lives by making a decision to believe the allowers instead.

1. "Take your time."
2. "It's OK to please yourself also."
3. "It's OK to feel."
4. "Do it."
5. "Do your best."

Changing your life will probably mean you will become more aware of your feelings than you have been before. Feelings can help or hurt you. The next section will show you how important your feelings are.

Section Two

You and Your Feelings

Are you in touch with your feelings: rarely, frequently, often? When you were born, you knew exactly how you were feeling all the time—and you let the people around you know it. In "Child Development" (Part Two), we talk about babies and how they let their caretakers know when they are angry, scared, sad, hungry, cold, etc. In the "Injunctions" chart (p. 139) we listed two about feelings: 1) "Don't feel" and 2) "Don't show your feelings." We wish no one would ever give those messages to any child, but unfortunately many people have these messages firmly ingrained in their minds and therefore are seldom, if ever, in touch with their feelings. Being cut off from the feeling part of us means that we are cut off from one of the richest human qualities, and although we go on being alive in our bodies we are separated from our inner selves.

Becoming a person, in the true sense of that word, is a process of becoming more and more conscious of one's inner life and of taking responsibility for one's feelings and ensuing behavior. As therapists, we know that feelings can hurt us or they can help us as we allow ourselves to be aware and conscious. In this section, we talk about the basic human feelings of anger, sadness, fear, guilt, depression, anxiety, and being overwhelmed. An additional section discusses forgiveness, which although not feeling, is what must happen after one has dealt with one's guilt, and grief, which is a process involving many feelings.

As you go through this section about various feelings, we suggest that you read slowly and ask yourself how you behave when you have any of the feelings we talk about. Next, ask yourself if your behavior sometimes gets you into trouble, either with yourself or with others. Then, if you want to change the way you act, see what we have written that will be of help to you. Remember that all feelings are part of being human. Never deny any of them. The real thing each of us must take charge of is how we behave as a result of our feelings. In this book you have read the stories of a number of people who acted inappropriately in response to their feelings. Then they wrote about how through self-awareness, therapy, and hard work they changed their behavior. You can do the same.

"I'm Mad"

Most of us don't want someone else to be "mad" at us and most of us don't like it when we are "mad" at other people. We may avoid saying "mad" by using words such as "annoyed," "irritated," "hurt," "edgy," "short fused," or "angry," and thereby fool ourselves into believing we're not "mad." But our bodies and our minds know. Why all this uneasiness and discomfort about feeling "mad"? Why do we have to trick ourselves by hiding our true feelings, even from ourselves?

The answer to these questions probably lies in how we were taught by our parents. Many parents are uncomfortable around anger because they themselves have been taught by their parents that anger is bad. "If you're mad, don't show it" is the message. Probably this all got started when someone thought being mad meant hurting oneself or other people. And of course that's what actually took place in primitive societies. Somewhere, however, man learned that anger and destructiveness need not go together. There are safe ways to release anger, ways in which no one is harmed. Later on in this chapter we will list several ways in which this can be done. For now we want to talk about how anger manifests itself in behavior.

1. Anger toward other people is expressed physically, verbally, or psychologically.
   a. Physical abusers hit, push, scratch, murder, drive dangerously, vandalize, or wage war.
   b. Verbal abusers snipe, are overly argumentative, "hit below the belt," project negatively.
   c. Psychological abusers dominate, ignore, reject, insult, devour, lie, or are sarcastic.
2. Anger toward yourself is also expressed either physically, verbally, or psychologically.
   a. Examples of physical abuse are eating disorders (eating too little food, possibly resulting in anorexia nervosa, or eating too much food, possibly resulting in bulimia); substance abuse; working too much, making oneself ill; committing suicide.
   b. Verbal abuse: telling yourself bad things about yourself.
   c. Psychological abuse: feeling inadequate, unworthy, "one down."
3. Anger toward the environment results in one or more of the following: arson, vandalism, littering, destroying endangered species of animals or birds, and cruelty to animals.

Physical harm to oneself, another person, or the environment is never OK, but unless we know other ways to express our anger, we will go on harming someone or something.

Of all these kinds of abuse, physical abuse is usually easily recognized. Verbal abuse is more subtle, but we often know when we have hurt others unfairly and we usually are aware when someone has hurt us. Psychological abuse is rather hard to spot because it is often not done consciously. Let's look at some examples.

1. George's mother always wanted to play the violin, but because her family was poor they could never afford to pay for vio-

lin lessons. Married to a physician, she became financially comfortable, but was unhappy in her marriage. George became her "darling." He was to have everything and be everything to his mother. Although George wanted to become an engineer, his mother decided he was to become a concert violinist, or at least a professional violinist. Obediently, George worked hard at his music. He became only a mediocre violinist, however, and because he earned only a small amount for his teaching, he had to take extra jobs in order to support himself. He never married, but George the violinist made his mother happy. She lived through his career. She was so unaware of how she had dominated her son that she honestly thought that George had wanted this career. George was too frightened to admit how unhappy he was. He died at forty-six. No one knew why.

2. Betsy was an active, imaginative, fearless and happy child. Her mother had been a shy, frightened, and quiet child. She was puzzled and overwhelmed by Betsy's energy, and perhaps envious of her daughter's free spirit. This all translated into negativity. Nothing Betsy could do was "right" except earning her excellent school grades. Betsy soon learned that there was no pleasing her mother. She thought "it was all her fault," "she was the bad one," her mother must be right. Betsy worked for the one thing she could do well. She had dreams inside her she never shared—dreams of poetry and music. (These things were not practical, her mother told her.) Betsy decided to become a college professor. She had a brilliant career and was respected in her community. Underneath all her outward success, however, she suffered untold agony because she still believed what she had learned when she was little. She never did it right. She was bad. There was something wrong with her. She really believed herself to be an unworthy and unlovable person.

3. Caroline was a pretty, charming, and very intelligent woman married to Phil, a handsome yuppie who was lionized by most women and adored by his mother and sisters. Men admired his business clout and his shrewd dealings in the stock market. Phil seemed to overshadow Caroline by a thousand leagues. Whenever Caroline had an idea, Phil had a better one. Whenever Caroline

suggested something, Phil had already thought of better arrangements and had gone ahead without consulting her. Caroline couldn't even raise the children properly. Phil and his mother knew better. After years of marriage, Caroline had learned to hide in her protective shell, tell herself she was a failure as a wife, a mother, and a person, and finally plan ways to kill herself.

George, Betsy, and Caroline were all abused psychologically by parents who were probably unaware of that abuse. If asked about how they were treating the children, they would probably have told us they were doing what was best for those in question, but they were all angry and were afraid to show that anger.

We wrote earlier that we would discuss ways of releasing anger that would not be harmful to ourselves or other people. The following suggestions may be used for past angers or for anger which is in the "now." Our counsel is to rid yourself of anger as quickly as possible so that you unblock your energy and free that energy for feelings that are more life-giving. Here are seven ideas for the safe release of "mad."

1. Exercise in whatever way you can—bike, swim, walk—whatever will use energy, get your blood flowing, and get oxygen into your system.

2. Place one or two pillows on your mattress or on a sturdy chair. Imagine the person you are angry with is on those pillows. Let yourself feel as "mad" as you honestly are and then begin to hit the pillow as hard as you can, imagining that you are hitting the person with whom you are so angry. While you are hitting, begin to yell out your anger. Keep your words short: "I hate you." "I'm mad." "I wish you were dead." "I hope I never see you again." "I'm mad at you, I'm mad at you, I'm mad at you!" Remember, anger is a Child feeling, and the more you hit and the louder you yell, the more the Child in you is expressed. Children do not go on being angry forever. Once they are allowed to express their true feelings, they will go from negative ones to positive ones. When your Child has "gotten it all out," then your Adult will figure out ways to solve the situation you are angry about.

3. Roll up a bath towel lengthwise and hit the floor as a variation of number 2.

Whenever you elect to use a hitting or pounding exercise, remember it is crucial that you actually feel anger in your body before you begin to hit. Strong emotions are powerful inside our bodies, and if that power is from negative emotions, it can hurt us physically and emotionally. Anger power needs to be discharged so that we can recharge our bodies with energy of another kind—energy to care about others and to have warm, loving relationships with them.

4. Tear up an old telephone book or magazine and yell out your "mad" while you're doing the tearing.

5. Find a pile of stones out of doors and throw them as hard as you can into the water, against the side of an old building or anywhere where they won't hurt anything of value.

6. Get some big piece of paper such as unprinted newsprint and then with a large crayon scribble all the angry words and phrases you can think of. At the same time, yell out the words you are scribbling.

7. Get some child's play dough. Make an image of the person you are angry with. Then pull off the legs and arms and throw the pieces against a basement or garage wall while telling the person how much you hate him (her).

If you, dear reader, are shocked by all this violence, remember that we are offering ways for you to release safely the anger and rage you already feel within you.

Release of anger gets the poison out of you and frees you to return to a life without rancor. Freed of anger, you are then free to solve the problem that sparked the anger in the first place.

One final word: It is important to decide before we give up any strong negative emotion what other emotion we want to put in its place. In the case of anger, you might ask yourself, "What would I rather do than to be mad"? Some options are: 1) having good relationships with..., 2) feeling good inside myself that I am no longer spending time being mad and sulking, 3) laughing because it was all a misunderstanding, 4) learning to love myself instead of dumping on myself, 5) enjoying nature rather than taking my "mad" out on it. The point is to finish up feeling good about yourself and other people and being alive. Everyone has a right to stay "mad" as long as they want to. Some people find it more fun to get on with life and enjoy themselves.

"I'm Bad"

A feeling of guilt is one of the primary reasons for entering therapy. Other words for guilt are embarrassment, shame, remorse, unworthiness, worthlessness, unforgiveableness. These are all grown up words. The little child says simply, "I'm bad."

Unfortunately, many people are unaware of the guilt feelings they have pushed away and forgotten. They deny them and cover them up with a variety of other behaviors such as:

1. Eating too much or not enough
2. Substance abuse
3. Exploiting others: sexually, physically, or psychologically (child or spouse abuse)
4. Talking too much or not enough
5. Overspending
6. Excessive travel

When people are unaware of their real feelings, they rarely seek help with their discomfort, preferring to blame others for their bad moods. However, when a person becomes conscious of his (her) discomfort and is willing to take responsibility for change, then a major first step has been taken. If that person finds a competent therapist, help is on the way. New ways of living can be learned.

The first thing that needs to be determined when dealing with guilt is whether the guilt is neurotic or realistic. The feeling is the same. The source is the real question. If I have stolen, abused another, lied, or cheated, I ought to feel guilty. If I feel no guilt, that in itself would be cause for therapeutic treatment. Character disorders and psychopathic personalities feel no guilt.

If, on the other hand, I feel guilty because I have spent money on myself, taken a vacation, had some fun after my day's work, stood up for my opinions, asked for something I needed, said "No" when imposed upon, these guilt feelings are what are called "neurotic guilt." I have learned to feel guilt because my parents or other important adults have taught me that these things are wrong, when in reality they are simply ways of taking care of myself.

If I suffer from neurotic guilt, I need help to overcome my neurosis. Many people can help themselves by using the following guidelines:

1. At birth, you were given the right to experience all feelings—joy, sadness, fear, excitement, anger, etc.

2. You were born OK—good, beautiful in your person, worthwhile.

3. You are responsible only for your own behavior, not that of your parents, children, or spouse.

4. Mistakes are learning opportunities, not guilt trips.

5. Money is to use, share, and enjoy.

6. Be as good to yourself as you are to others.

7. Work a reasonable day (8 hours), then stop.

8. Be kind to children, old people, the disadvantaged and disabled, and animals.

If you still experience neurotic guilt after putting these eight truths into your behavior, then it would be a good idea for you to find a competent therapist.

If your guilt is not neurotic, you need to stop doing whatever you're doing that causes the guilt, and then you need to ask forgiveness from the person(s) you have wronged. If you are a religious person, you need to ask forgiveness from God. The matter is then settled. Sorrow, forgiveness asked for, forgiveness given, behavior changed, guilt removed—that is the sequence.

As therapists, the authors are surprised by the number of peo-

ple who tell us they are religious and yet go on burdened with
guilt. They can talk about the truths of religion in terms of guilt
and forgiveness, but they are unwilling or unable to believe in forgiveness for themselves. In such instances, our counsel is simply
this: If you believe in God and you believe God forgives, then con-
fess your sin, ask God's forgiveness, make it right with the one(s)
you have wronged, and then do what God does: let your guilt go
and forgive yourself. If you find that you are unable or unwilling
to forgive yourself, then we advise you also find a competent
therapist.

"I'm Scared"

In Western culture, it is usually all right for a little girl to be
scared and show her feelings, but a little boy is supposed to be "a
big man." Scared may be translated into "afraid," "terror-
stricken," "petrified" (a major scare), but usually "scared" is simply called "scared."

How do we act and what do we do when we are scared?

1. Within ourselves, our feelings are those of being inadequate,
helpless, hopeless, or immobilized, and we often look for someone to rescue us from our real or imagined persecutor.

2. We make ourselves ill with diarrhea, muscle tension, diges-
tive problems, headaches, overeating, smoking, sleeping, or taking drugs.

3. We withdraw from people, hide away or frequently change
jobs, houses, friends, or spouses.

4. We underachieve in our activities.

5. We deny our scare by covering it over with another feeling,
usually anger, but sometimes sadness.

When we are scared, we become like little children waiting for
a big mommy or daddy to protect us and get rid of whatever is
scaring us.

The problem with scare in grown-up men and women is that

unless there is an obvious and objective reason for the fear (earth-quake, illness, threat of war), we are reluctant to let others know that we are frightened. We have a hunch that being scared is childish and that we are old enough to have outgrown it, or at least to handle our fear ourselves. This kind of thinking keeps us locked inside ourselves and solves nothing. It is a sure sign of strength to ask for help when we need it, and any overpowering feeling can be resolved if we learn how to take care of ourselves. One of the ways to do this is to seek help from others when we need it. Dr. Harry Overstreet's *Overcoming Fear in Ourselves and Others* is a book you may want to read for some down-to-earth suggestions.

The authors have counseled many people who tell us about their fears. Often this is a cry for help, and we are the only people they have confided in. The first thing we try to find out is whether the fear is objective, that is, whether it is related to an object that would produce fear in most people or is just in this person. Objec-tive fear can be caused by falling, losing one's memory, terminal illness, surgery, death (one's own or a beloved's), beginning a new experience such as school or a new job, being attacked by an animal such as a dog or snake, and nuclear war. These and other similar things produce fear in most people.

Non-objective fear, on the other hand, is experienced as terrify-ing, but not by most people. This type of fear can be caused by go-ing to a party, riding in an elevator, train or airplane, going out-side of the house, or being spoken to by a stranger. None of these is fear-producing in themselves, but they are dreaded by some people.

If you have fears similar to this last list, chances are that your fears are based on early childhood experiences that have never been resolved. These fears can be diminished and usually disap-pear altogether. One way to accomplish this is by a writing exer-cise. Get in touch with an early childhood experience in which you first felt the kind of fear you now have. Let yourself live in that former happening. Feel whatever you felt then. Write your story as if it is happening now. Next, decide how you would like the story to have been so that you would not have been afraid.

Now rewrite the story with this happy ending and replace your old fear with this new and good feeling.

Here is an example of how this worked with one person. Mary dreaded parties. When she was invited to one, she told herself how awful it would be to go. When she went to a party, she would sit all alone, hoping no one would notice her, but at the same time envying other people who seemed to be having a good time. When she returned home, she would feel miserable because she had indeed had a bad time, and then she would use this occasion to confirm again her decision that parties were scary and that she would never go to another one.

When Mary came to therapy, we asked her to do the writing exercise after we had talked with her about her fears. When Mary wrote, she remembered a birthday party when she was five years old. In a child's game she had by accident hurt a little boy with a sharp garden tool which fell on his head and cut a deep gash that bled profusely. Mary was horrified at what "she had done," then told herself she was a bad girl and that if she hadn't come to the party, Billy wouldn't have been hurt. The last part was true, but not the first. Mary had not purposely "done" a bad thing. She had had an accident. She was not "a bad girl."

Her decision to dread parties was how she punished herself. But Mary hadn't deserved to be punished in the first place. No adult had talked with her and helped her to see all this. Perhaps she had never told anyone how scared she felt. But when Mary wrote the incident down and we talked about it, she was able to see that she was not bad, never should have punished herself, and she could, if she chose, go to parties as a grown-up person, enjoy people, and have fun. Mary decided to do just that.

There are other deep fears which are not as simple as Mary's to heal. These deeper fears may be phobias. Healing a phobia is not simple because fear that can be named, fear of flying for instance, may be a cover-up for an unknown and unconscious fear, a kind of smoke screen we have put up to defend ourselves against the pain of recognition.

An example here may be helpful. John was afraid to fly and would admit it, but since flying was essential for his business he had to fly often. As a grown-up man, John thought he couldn't tell anyone for fear of being called sissy. Now he had two fears. So rather than deal with either, John just flew, white-knuckled, on and on. He tried the martini cure—a few drinks to ease his terror, but he was still scared stiff every mile of every flight. Sober or "martini-ized," John was convinced that the plane would never get up, wouldn't stay up when it gained its final altitude, and would certainly end up in a crash landing. John's head knew all the facts about air travel being safer than automobiles, the ratio of flights and passenger numbers to accidents, etc., but John's stomach believed none of it. Year after year, John endured.

One day he came to therapy about his phobia. The course of his therapy is too long to write about here, but the turning point came when we discovered that John was suicidal. His death would, he thought, solve the problem of being rejected by his mother, a rejection he had experienced in his unconscious at the time of his birth, and perhaps even prenatally. His mother had never wanted a child, had become pregnant without planning for a child, and had cut John off emotionally from the beginning. His mother had no conscious knowledge of her own feelings and tried to be a good mother, but her rejection was communicated to her son from the first.

As is natural for children who experience rejection from a parent, John decided that he must be bad and that something must really be the matter with him. His Child decision, then, was also a natural one. He would get rid of himself and his mother would be happy when he was no longer around. This decision was, of course, made subconsciously by John when he was very small. He became conscious of all this in therapy as he recorded his dreams and we worked on them together to understand the message from his unconscious mind to his now struggling self. It was quite clear that for years John had been suicidal, and now he recalled times when he had plans to kill himself.

John worked hard to incorporate a new Parent inside himself, to substitute caring and loving messages about himself for the old destructive "You bother me. You're a burden, I don't want you here." When he realized that from his birth and throughout his life he had been and was now lovable and worthwhile, John saw that his thoughts of suicide had been an attempt to take care of his mother's neurosis. His fear of flying had been a veiled cover-up of his suicidal thoughts, and when he no longer was suicidal he no longer feared flying. John was able to forgive his mother for her rejection of him, since she herself had been rejected by her own parents and never meant consciously to harm her son. He was able to stop living for his mother inside his own head and start living for himself as a grown-up person. He became an enthusiastic traveler, and when he retired, he took exciting trips all over the world—no martinis, no white knuckles, no fear—only fun.

Both Mary and John are examples of how fear blocks our energy flow. Mary used her energy to scare herself about parties. John used energy to keep himself miserable on his business trips. When they were willing to face their fears and discover the skeletons in their closets, their energy was available for more fun: parties for Mary, vacation travel for John.

If you suffer from fears which are not caused by objective things, here are some ways you can unblock your energy when you are afraid.

1. Do what Mary did. Write about your fear. Choose an incident as early in your life as you remember, one that ties in with the fear you feel today. As you write, you may recall an even earlier experience. Write as often as you like, be honest, face into it. Then rewrite the story with a happier ending, one in which you feel happy, secure, and relaxed.

2. Use a doll, stuffed animal, or pillow, as we suggested in the section on sadness and anger. Let the doll, animal, or pillow representing your inner Child, tell you all about her (his) scare. Then you, as a very loving Parent, tell your inner Child how you will take care of her (him) from now on whenever she (he) has that same fear, or any other fear.

3. Draw your fear or use clay forms to represent your fear. Get in touch with your deep feelings. Then parent as in 2 above.

4. Fantasize. Let your imagination create a time and place when you felt secure and safe. Picture the scene in your mind just as if it were happening now. Bring in whomever you choose and

whatever you choose to create a warm, safe place for your inner Child. Some people choose lovely outdoor places such as meadows, beaches, hilltops; other people build cocoons around them, bubbles, space ships, shelters of all kinds. Bring in a big brother or sister, a loving friend, a beloved parent, whoever will be protective and caring. Stay in the place with the person or people you have chosen as long as you need to feel trust and confidence instead of fear.

Remember that most often when we are fearful, we have scared ourselves. Most children do this when they are three years old. The bear in the closet, the ogre under the bed are real when we are three. Good mommies and daddies don't laugh at us; they tell us they will always take care of us no matter what, and then they show us the safety of the closet or the bed. We did all this when we were three; we don't need to continue to scare ourselves.

"I'm Sad"

Most of us want to get away from a person who is angry, but a sad person evokes our comfort and concern. Sadness has a way of pulling at our heart strings; all but the most hardened of us want to help ease pain if we can.

In "Child Development" (Part Two) we talk about real feelings and "rackets": real feelings—those appropriate to circumstances; rackets—those "cover ups" we learn to "put on" early in life in order to get something in a "rip-off" way. When we see someone who is sad or when we experience sadness in ourselves, we need to have an accurate understanding of the difference between real feelings and rackets. Racket sadness is a way to manipulate others into feeling sorry for us so that they will give us something we would not otherwise be given. For instance, if I want a new car and my husband has said we can't afford it, I may become very sad, knowing that my tears will get me what I want. I may cry pathetically, and then he may tell me I can buy the car and he will find a way to pay for it. If I ask to get off early from work and my boss doesn't want me to, I may look very helpless and hurt, so that he will feel guilty enough to tell me it's OK and to take the time off. Racket sadness is destructive to ourselves and others because it is manipulative and dishonest.

Here are some of the things to look for in yourself and other people to detect racket sadness:

1. In relationship to other people, "racket" people
   a. sit in corners and look rejected
   b. feel persecuted: "It is his (her, their) fault."
   c. look for a "rescuer," fairy godmother, the key to the magic garden, the Prince, the Princess
   d. are self-centered and egocentric in conversation
2. In relationship to themselves, they
   a. cut themselves down
   b. refuse to accept strokes from other people
   c. turn down what they can have because they want something else
   d. sap their own energy by pouting
   e. withdraw
   f. play the Victim: "I'm just a beggar. Put a penny in my cup"
   g. waste time
   h. act the martyr
   i. make themselves ill
   j. stop eating or overeat, overindulge in smoking, medication, sleeping, or drugs.

The problem in relating to people who are in racket sadness is that they always believe their suffering is objectively caused and, when we will not be hooked into their misery, they try their best to send us on a "guilt trip." Unless we are very wise, we often let ourselves feel guilty, but then back down and give them whatever they wanted. How many young women have not gone out with fine young men because mother becomes ill whenever they have a date?

Telling the difference between genuine sadness and manipulative sadness is not easy, but it can be done. Here's an example of the way two different women handled the death of their husbands. Marjorie's husband, fourteen years older than she, died two years ago. After a year of sadness, grief, and loss, Marjorie moved out of her big house to a retirement village. The next year someone asked her how she was getting on. Marjorie replied, "We were married fifty-one years. We had a wonderful life together. What more can anyone ask? I miss Herb very much, but life has to go on, and even though there are lonely times, I am happy with my friends and hobbies and volunteer work." Clearly Marjorie's sadness has been faced, worked through, and dealt with appropriately.

Mary, on the other hand, lets everyone she meets know that she is a widow who lost her husband twelve years ago. She stays depressed because she dwells on her aloneness, lamenting that everyone else has someone to be with them. She relives and retells Ken's death at each anniversary, wondering how she can go on living. It is interesting that while Ken was alive she was often angry with him and complained about her unhappy marriage. The purpose of Mary's sadness seems to be to get everyone to feel sorry for her and to occupy their time talking about her. Whenever she learns about someone else's problems she says that they are not as painful as hers. No one else's suffering really matters. Mary has taken her grief of many years ago and hung on to it in order to get attention from everyone she knows. She would rather keep her racket of sadness than to give it up. She likes to be at the center of things. She likes people to feel sorry for her. Hers is a real racket, and when people move away from her, as they always do, she says they don't care. It never occurs to Mary that she has a problem.

The next time you are sad, ask yourself, "Am I sad because I have a real loss, or am I feeling and acting sad in order to manipulate other people?" If the latter is true, ask yourself how you can get your own needs met in an honest way. You may have a message in your head that tells you you always have to be strong and therefore it's not okay for you to ask for help. If you put yourself down in this way, then perhaps the only way you know of to be cared for is to act sad and helpless. We'd like to suggest that you teach yourself that it is okay for you to ask for what you want directly. You don't have to act like a little beggar in order to get your needs met.

You may have had a parent who was usually sad. You may be imitating him or her and not know that it's okay for you to have fun and enjoy yourself. You don't have to go on keeping this parent company. People who are habitually "misery packets" usually get left alone. If you've been a misery packet for most of your life, you can begin to change right now and trade in your sadness for joy.

So much for sad rackets. Now, let's talk about what you can do the next time you are in touch with sadness over a genuine disappointment or loss. How can you begin to heal? Here are some suggestions:

1. Let yourself cry as often and as much as you need to.

2. Call a friend who, you know, cares about you and ask your friend to comfort you by telling you whatever he or she can say honestly. You may need to call many times and ask for help if your grief is because of a deep loss such as terminal illness, a broken engagement, finding out you cannot have a child, the death of a spouse, etc. Talking things out gives your friend a chance to comfort you, and gives you strength and support to bear your loss. If you hear a voice in your head saying, "Don't bother people with your troubles. You're grown up. Take care of yourself," tell these messages to go away then listen to other messages such as, "Ask for what you want and need. You have a right to be taken care of. You are loved. Let people help you."

3. If you have no one you can ask to comfort you, take a little doll or pillow to represent your own inner Child. Let that Child tell you about her (his) pain. Then as a good Parent, comfort your Child with messages of strength and support. Here are a few examples:

    a. "I know you're sad. Cry as much as you want to. Get it out and you'll feel much better."

    b. "It's hard to lose someone you love. You feel terribly lonely now. I'm glad you're in touch with your feelings. When you're ready, you can be with other people. They aren't the same as _____, but there are lots of people who love you and are your friends."

c. "The doctor has said you are dying, but you aren't dying in your spirit. That will live forever. I'll stick with you while your body dies, and I'll take care of you the best way I can. I'll be there with you after death, too."

4. Write about your sadness. Write exactly how you feel. No one else need read it, so pour your heart out. Write day after day and if you write just what you feel, you will gradually begin to heal. We have had many people do this and they all tell us that healing does take place, slowly but surely.

5. Draw your feelings of sadness. You are not trying to be an artist. Just draw as a child does. Don't think. Just feel. Draw on large unprinted newsprint with large kindergarten crayons. Draw, draw, and draw again. Healing will come gradually.

6. Trust that out of sadness eventually comes joy. They are two sides of the experience of being human.

One final word about feelings of sadness. Whenever they begin to heal and whenever they leave, we must decide what we want to feel in place of them. Any powerful feeling leaves a vacuum inside us when it leaves our psyche. We all have choices about what we want to feel. People who choose to hang on to negative feelings can spend their lives wasting their energy doing just that. People who want to live with positive energy can choose to feel those feelings which make for health and wholeness. Sadness can be replaced. We must decide. As with anger and fear, we may choose instead to feel love, joy, and peace.

"I'm Depressed"

Depression is so common in today's world that we hardly notice when someone tells us they are taking Elavil or Prozac or any one of the other "uppers." Our TV screens and our public press bombard us with a dreadful world. How can anyone help feeling "blue," "down," "bored," "flat," "hopeless," "helpless," "loveless"? People complain about being tired, or having no energy or interest: "Nothing matters, nobody cares." People who don't talk about their feelings will probably evidence their depression in their actions. They usually sigh a great deal, and are often passive (doing nothing to solve their problems). All systems seem very slow and heavy (walking, talking, etc.). They often have serious disturbances in eating, sleeping, and elimination. They frequently have thoughts of suicide. They will do a lot of living "yesterday" and focus what little energy they have on "how it was." They will spend time in rumination and excessive crying. They will pop the latest pill that promises relief from this awful torture, which in medieval times was called "melancholia." Popping pills will bring relief at first, but medication relieves only symptoms. It does nothing to get at the cause and to bring healing.

If you are depressed a great deal of the time or if you know someone else who is often depressed, we want you to know that depression—like other psychological pain—can be alleviated. Occasionally there are people who have organic brain damage or who have a serious chemical imbalance for which medication may be prescribed to alleviate depression. Also, depression which has not been worked through at an early stage may sometimes push people into violent behavior, so that they are dangerous to themselves or other people. Here again, medication may be used, but in such cases the medication should be only for crisis relief. It will give "time out," but it will do nothing to solve the cause of the depression. As soon as possible, depressed people need to begin to understand their depression and to solve whatever problems underlie it.

The first thing we suggest for people who are depressed is that they get moving: use some energy in running, fast walking, yelling, hitting safe objects, etc. The reason for this is that people who are depressed immobilize themselves and become more and more inert. Using energy is a quick way to break the inert cycle.

The next thing to understand about depression is that in most cases, depression is anger turned inward, on one's self. We teach that anger directed toward one's self is neither natural nor healthy.

Every newborn baby is a gift to the world. The baby reaches out to his caretaker in trust, need, and joy. If that innocence is met with appropriate warmth and love and the baby is cared for, he will grow up loving himself and those he meets. As he is taught what to do and what not to do for his own well-being and that of others, he will, of course, gradually learn how to become his own good caretaker. He will analyze his problems and find ways to solve them. He will not be angry with himself. If, on the other hand, he is mistaught, he will turn anger in on himself.

Some children are not permitted to show anger because the adults in their world are uncomfortable with anger. Adults should teach children in their care how to express anger appropriately, that is, without hurting themselves, other people, or things. If a child is not allowed to express anger appropriately, he will usually turn it in on himself. Anger is a part of life and needs to be owned, accepted, and expressed appropriately.

If we realize that in almost all instances, depression is anger turned inward, we can ask ourselves what we are really angry about and then focus on problem-solving rather than on hurting ourselves with our rage.

Many people find that they are depressed when they have not achieved a goal which they have set for themselves or which they have allowed someone else to set for them. School grades are a good example. A "B" student may be getting "C" grades. If the student or his parents knows that he can do better, he may set out to get a "B." When he receives the "B," instead of stroking himself and gaining praise from his parents, he may "get down" on himself because he didn't make an "A." "A's" are fine for "A" type students, but they must not be the goal of the student who lacks the ability to achieve that standard. Instead of being depressed, the "B" achiever needs to rejoice in having worked at his ability level, and not compare himself with "A" students. A second example: The man who achieves a fine position at middle-management level needs to reward himself for achieving a managerial position, not whip himself because someone else with more ability is in top management.

Many people feel depressed because of what they don't have instead of giving thanks for what they do have. This problem can occur in many areas, such as material possessions, appearance, position, travel, children, influence, etc. When a person retires from work, he or she often experiences depression shortly afterwards. This is especially true of people who "are what they do." If they are not working, they feel worthless. Other people experience depression when they move to a new house or a new community, even though they have chosen to make the move. They have left "the old" and they are not yet secure in "the new." Their depression often masks the more basic feeling of sadness. Many women become depressed after giving birth. Their babies are healthy and the women wanted them, but they are nonetheless depressed. This "post-partum" depression, if severe enough, may result in suicidal thinking and desperate moods of darkness.

Depression, then, is often a mask for anger that a person really feels toward someone or something. If I will look at the anger behind my mask and then begin to solve that problem, I will find that I am no longer depressed. In doing this, I must realize that I cannot change other people, and that there are many things about which I can do nothing. But once I face my anger I can stop hurting myself and I can change my attitude toward other people and situations. I can stop letting them destroy my peace of mind.

When depression is a mask for sadness, I can take the time to find out what I am sad about, begin to face into that sadness, and decide how I can begin to solve my problems. Perhaps I want to allow myself to be sad for some time. There is a time for grief and sadness. I can own that fact, but I do not then have to hurt myself with depression. If I accept that this is a time for sadness, I can honor that time and then go on doing whatever I need or choose, even though my heart is heavy.

Depression may be a cover-up for scare. Some people, especially men who have been laughed at or called "scaredy cats," have learned to cover up times of fearfulness. Again, in this case a person can know that fear is a part of living just like anger or sadness, and it can be owned and expressed instead of being allowed to turn into depression.

If you suspect that "mad," "sad," or "scared" feelings are beneath your depression, review the sections in this chapter that deal specifically with each of these feelings. Also, read again the stories of Sara and Amy to see how depression hurt these two women and how therapy freed them to use their energy to heal that depression.

"I'm Anxious"

Anxiety is a state of being apprehensive, worried, suspicious, or uneasy about something terrible that may happen. Anxiety differs from fear in that the trigger for it is scary thought rather than an actual event. For example, being unable to sleep in a hotel room lest someone break into the room is different from waking up to the sound of an intruder's careful movements and heavy breathing.

Anxious people are worried, afraid or panicky; they have doubts or misgivings about outcomes and are often suspicious. They feel uncomfortable and describe their sensations as follows:

"It's as if I can't swallow."
"I'm afraid I'll choke to death."
"I have butterflies in my stomach."
"I just want to get away from here."
"I'm fit to be tied."
"I'm scared to death."
"I'm petrified."
"I'm tied up in knots."
"I'm trembling all over."
"I'm about to explode."
"I'm about to faint."
"I'm afraid I'll fall apart."
"I'm going around in circles."

Anxiety is frequently manifested by gasping for breath, holding one's breath, hyperventilating, or agitation. It involves much undirected and non-problem-solving activity. Anxious people have difficulty making decisions or starting a task; sometimes they move on to other tasks without completing any of them. They may be discouraged, paralyzed or petrified, or preoccupied with the future. They may have disturbances with eating, sleeping, and elimination.

In "Child Development" (Part Two) we describe how children develop racket feelings when they find they are safer or they are getting a better response with rackets than with expressing natural feelings. Anxiety itself is a racket; sometimes it can be used instead of anger or instead of thinking. In fact, the most common mechanism used as a rationalization for non-thinking and non-problem-solving behavior is anxiety. Anxiety is a feeling we learn to have as a result of scaring ourselves in our own heads. The kinds of phrases we use to do this include, "You'd better look out." "You'll get caught." "What will they think?"

For example, James was angry because he had to do his homework when he wanted to be playing with his friends. He decided to rush through it as quickly as he could. The next day he was reprimanded by his teacher in front of his classmates for making so many mistakes. He hated that and saw a smirk on another boy's face. The next time he had arithmetic homework, all he remembered was the smirk on the boy's face and the teacher's sarcasm. Instead of reminding himself that he was good with numbers, and all he needed to do was to take care and double-check his work, he started to scare himself about how awful it would be if that ever happened again. He sat and "stewed."

After a time, his mother asked him why he was taking so long over his work. He played helpless, and she did his sums for him. Getting anxious instead of finding out how to solve his problem worked that night and many other times at home. It was not long before he started to convince himself in class that he'd better look out or he might make mistakes there. His grades deteriorated and his mother spent more and more time helping him at home. He learned, "If I worry enough, someone will help me." As a grown man James inhibited himself greatly for fear he would make mistakes. He married a woman who was domineering and threatened him as if he were a little boy. Although his mother had the best of intentions, her babying James had not been helpful. What he needed to learn was to stop scaring himself and to think.

The major characteristic of anxiety is that it is accompanied by a "what if." What if:

"I lose my job."
"The plane crashes."
"I fail."
"No one loves me."
"I miss the train."
"They rip me off."
"There's not enough money?"

The list can go on for pages. Whatever the "what if" is, when people scare themselves about the future the result is anxiety and threat.

Whenever there is any threat, breathing changes. Generally, people respond to threat by gasping and then holding their breath. This is then followed either by continued slowed-down breathing, panting, or hyperventilation. Whatever the change, the result is an imbalance of oxygen in the lungs and then in the blood stream, causing stress and discomfort which, in turn, aggravate the problem.

Anxiety is one of the most frequent problems people present when they come for psychotherapy. There are four main categories, each of which can vary from mild to debilitating. They are: 1) anxiety as a way of life; 2) anxiety in the face of specific events; 3) anxiety which is repressed and then manifested in physical symptoms; 4) panic attacks.

People who make anxiety a way of life may be like Rodney who was a "worry wart," or Judy, who paralyzed herself with her apprehensions. Rodney always had something to keep himself from being at peace with himself. If he wasn't concerned about his taxes, it was his health, his children, his car, a possible hurricane, or his golf game. No one took his concerns too seriously, and he had no serious setbacks. The saddest thing was that he was his own worst enemy and never had time to relax or to have any fun.

Judy had a high level of anxiety. When she began therapy she said she had always had a long list of worries. She then worried about which problems she should tackle first and thereby added another one to her list. She started to do things but never finished them. She could not keep a job, her house was a shambles, and she became more and more distressed. The situation was so bad that her husband was threatening to leave.

People who experience anxiety around specific events are often free from the problem most of the time. Bill was a fun-loving and carefree man in almost all aspects of his life. He was a most effective sales manager. However, when he knew he was going to have to speak in public he put himself through torment. He kept himself awake worrying about forgetting his notes, trembling with fear, losing his voice, and the like for nights at a time. Before he began, his hands sweated and he could feel his heart beating as if he had just run five miles. He was absolutely sure he'd make a fool of himself. He never did, but that did not stop him worrying the next time.

People who suffer from phobias are extremely anxious in the face of their feared situations. Some people have one phobia, others have several. There is a myth that it is useless to work with people toward giving up a phobia because they will find another one to take its place. We have found that to be untrue. For example, in Part One, Timothy's mother explains how he was able to solve his panic and fear about leaving his parents.

An example of a mild form of repressing anxiety and developing a symbolic physical problem is Paul. He was nauseated whenever his supervisor came for his semi-annual visits. After talking about the situation for just a few minutes he said, "I just can't stomach that man." He did not realize what he'd said until I asked him to repeat that statement two or three times. Then he laughed and said, "Hmm! I guess I know how to get rid of him!"

In their stories, Connie and Krys tell of ways they converted their anxieties into physical symptoms—Connie with her inability to swallow and Krys with her hysterical blindness. Both of these somatizations were serious and needed medical attention.

Maude, who was twenty-five when she first came for therapy, was having frequent panic attacks. She could never predict when they would come. They had begun about five years before. Initially she had one every few months; now she was having one every few days. She described the attacks as onslaughts which suddenly descended upon her. At the moment of the attack she felt dizzy, sweated profusely, and could not breathe. The most scary thing was that she felt sure that she would never get enough breath and that she'd die.

People who have minor problems with anxiety can do much to help themselves by learning how to change the way they talk to themselves in their own heads. If you are one of these people, the next time you feel anxious tell yourself, "Stop scaring yourself! Give yourself a moment to think!" Then ask yourself, "What can I do to solve the problem now?" Then do that. If you are interested in a more detailed account of how to change the way you talk to yourself, there is a whole chapter on the subject in our book, *Aging with Joy*.

Those who have phobias and/or are experiencing physical problems as a result of having been anxious can be helped through psychotherapy. Amy, Krys, Heather, Barbara, and several others of those who have told their stories in this book had problems with anxiety. We have a prescription for anyone who has panic or anxiety attacks. If you follow our plan you may be able to cure yourself. Practice this procedure once a day for at least a week so that if ever you have another attack you will know exactly what to do. Here it is:

1. Sit down.

2. Grab something and hold it firmly (if there's nothing handy, grab your arm).

3. Exhale as much as possible. A good way to do this is to sing, "Ooooooo" for as long as you can.

4. Inhale (you'll do this naturally).

5. Concentrate on your breathing for a while. Do this until you are breathing deeply and evenly.

6. Look around the room. Notice what you see. Particularly notice colors and shapes.

7. Check carefully to see if there is anything scary where you are. (It's almost certain there'll be nothing.) If there is, e.g., if a

mouse runs across the room and you're afraid of mice—do something about it and then check it out again to make sure there's nothing scary there.

8. Talk to yourself (aloud if you wish) and tell yourself: "Good, you're breathing well now." "I know how to take care of you." "There's nothing to be afraid of now."

Whenever we have taught this process to people with panic attacks, they have found that it serves two purposes. First, it gives them a tool to use in case of an attack. Second, it relieves their fear and anxiety about having another attack and not knowing what to do. At least 50 percent of our people have felt so much relief in knowing that they no longer have to fear not knowing what to do if they have another attack, that they never have one. Those who have experienced further attacks have reported that they have been minor.

The reason people feel as if they cannot breathe when they have panic attacks is that the more anxious they become, the more they hold their "old" breath and the less room there is in their lungs to inhale. The problem is not an inability to breathe, it is an inhibition against exhaling. The reason for holding something and concentrating on what is in the room is a simple way to get back into the here and now. Anxiety and living in the present are mutually exclusive.

"I'm Overwhelmed"

A television commercial done with speeded-up camera shows Mom trying to get five kids into her car while the kids keep running around doing one more thing before she corrals them. At home and exhausted from her day, Mom is out of breath and looks up to see Dad coming in saying, "What did you do all day, Honey?" Another commercial, this one advertising a new computer, shows a typical office without a computer, again with a speeded-up camera, everyone in the company racing from office to office getting the day's work done in frantic fashion. Both Mom and the office personnel are obviously overwhelmed.

When people feel overwhelmed they are often on a "high" and don't realize they are doing too much. They say things such as "Life's just great, really just great," or "I'm really on top, really on top," or "I can handle anything. Just give it to me." On the other hand, people who are aware of being overwhelmed may say, "I'm worried sick," "I'm scared to death," "It's all too much," "I can't do anything." Thus, people who are overwhelmed whether they are aware of it or not, are overexcited, overelated, high, manic, spaced out, stressed out, or pressured.

Those who are overwhelmed often behave in ways that begin to get them into trouble with themselves and other people. Some examples: 1) speeding, 2) overdrawn checking accounts, 3) extravagant purchases, 4) impulsive decisions, 5) impulsive activity, 6) non-thinking behavior, 7) disturbances in eating, sleeping, elimination, 8) passivity (doing nothing to solve problems), 9) ruminating, 10) going around in circles, "The hurrier I go, the behinder I get," 11) acting martyred and seeking sympathy, 12) starting many things, but not finishing most of them.

Most of us have sympathy for people who are overwhelmed, perhaps because we ourselves have felt just like that at times. Being overwhelmed seems to be part of the human condition in our day. Many of us are out of breath and have no time even for the things we say we want to do. Of course there is little harm in being busy and in working or playing hard, but that is not the same thing as being overwhelmed. Being overwhelmed is being out of control and being caught up in grandiosity, seeing oneself as either all-powerful or all-helpless. How then can we help ourselves? Here are some suggestions which many people have found useful:

1. Ask yourself why you feel overwhelmed. Many people make use of having too much to do as a protection against having free time. Somehow, having free time (nothing to do) is frightening to them. They have probably been raised on a work ethic and have no permission to be free to enjoy and to do something other than work. If you are overwhelmed as a protection from this fear, we

invite you to be good to yourself and to give yourself permission to do a good day's work and then relax and enjoy yourself.

2. Think. No matter what you feel, you can think and make decisions slowly and wisely.

3. Slow down. There are very few times when you need to hurry. Allow extra time for each task and allow time between tasks.

4. Solve each problem as you come to it. Don't let them pile up. See "Problem Solving" chart on page 137.

5. If you need information or help, ask for it. You don't have to do everything alone.

6. Take care of your body and health by getting plenty of rest, nourishing food, exercise, and fun.

7. Remember: Your worth is not in what you do. Your worth is in who you are. Take time to "be," not just "do."

Forgiveness

Forgiveness seems to be in short supply in our modern world. Anger seems to be plentiful. We are not saying that everyone is angry, but we are aware that newspapers, magazines, and a great many television programs highlight angry people, angry groups, angry nations. It's as if many people see the world as hostile and decide the only way to survive is to protect themselves by being angry and showing it. Whites rage at blacks and blacks rage at whites. Labor attacks management and management finds ways to squeeze labor. Teens flaunt their rebellion against adult society, and adults blame teens for drugs, violence, and sexual license. Powerful nations blame developing countries for overpopulation, inertia, and disease. Developing countries blame first-world nations for polluting the environment, enslaving the poor, and exploiting their lands. Democratic countries blame Communist countries for not wanting peace and Communist countries blame democracies for talking peace and preparing for war in the name of national security. Anger does seem to be a way of life for many people.

Whatever happened to forgiveness? Why is it in such short

supply? To find an answer to our question, we need to remind ourselves that forgiveness is not natural to man, that is, man in his natural state. The natural state of man is to take care of himself, to fight for what he needs, to remember and seek revenge on those who interfere with his fulfillment of those needs. If we are looking for forgiveness, it is not to be found with natural man, but rather is a quality which man learns from the teachings of religion. In Christianity we encounter forgiveness as a principal teaching. Jesus, quoting the Jewish law of his day, says to his followers, "Ye have heard it said of old 'an eye for an eye and a tooth for a tooth'; but I say unto you, love your enemies and pray for them that despitefully use you." Again and again Jesus instructs his followers to practice forgiveness. Unfortunately, this is not what we find in practice. For great numbers of Christians, religion has little to do with what goes on in "the real world." Biblical teaching and words on Sunday are all well and good for church-going, but "one has to be practical and deal with the world in ways the world understands." Unfortunately for those who would like to get out from under the firm teachings of the faith, this is not so. Christianity is meant for the "real world," and the teaching about forgiveness in that world is perfectly clear. We are to forgive our enemies seventy times seven; in other words, always. We are to leave the matter of justice in God's hands and not be our brother's judge. The relationship between this kind of love and the matter of ethics has always been a difficult question, but Christianity is unequivocal on the matter of forgiveness. Unfortunately, the gap between the teaching of Jesus and the practice of his followers is embarrassing. This gap is what has happened to forgiveness among many of us.

When we ask what the teaching of Judaism is in regard to forgiveness, we must look at two answers. One is the answer in the Torah (the sacred teaching of the Law), and the other the teaching of the great literary Prophets. The teaching about forgiveness is not identical in these two sources. Judaism for the most part has followed the earlier concept of justice, that of the Torah. Here the teaching is "An eye for an eye and a tooth for a tooth." The Prophets, on the other hand, taught the forgiveness of one's enemies. To love God was to love his creatures, and as Yahweh had again and again forgiven Israel, so now Israel was to forgive her enemies. Later Judaism chose to follow the earlier teaching rather than that of the Prophets. One wonders if the problems of modern Israel are not a logical outcome of the "eye for an eye" position.

The Western world has for thousands of years given its religious adherence mainly to Christianity, and when we ask what has happened to forgiveness we must conclude that through the gradual erosion of religious practice, this most generous of attitudes has eroded also. If we look at forgiveness in terms of the human psyche, we realize how profound was the teaching of Jesus; for it is the lack of forgiveness, and thereby the holding on to anger, that is destructive to the psyche of modern man. This same truth is attested to by modern medicine as it shows us the destruction of our physical selves because of retained anger.

As therapists we have found what other therapists have found, that the greatest percentage of people who come to us come with the burden of guilt—guilt because they do not really know about forgiveness for themselves and for others. Generally, people do not come in and tell us they are experiencing guilt. They are aware of their depression, their anxiety, and sometimes their anger, sadness, and fear. Nonetheless, it becomes clear rather quickly that for most people there is an underlying feeling of guilt.

Invariably, we see the close tie between feelings of guilt and feelings of resentment. Forgiveness of oneself or another is virtually impossible as long as a person is filled with anger and resentment. One of the problems we face when we talk with people who are genuinely religious is that often their understanding of religion has served to increase their burdens of guilt. It would seem that many clergy preach on the wages of sin but do not emphasize enough the forgiveness of sin. A second problem arises from the fact that religious people are admonished to forgive others, but no one has helped them first deal with their anger so that they *can* forgive themselves and others.

In treatment, then, the first way we work is to help people identify their anger. Anger at whom? Anger at what? Then we help them learn how to pour all that old anger out, ridding themselves of the stockpile they have hung on to for so long. We teach them how to dump their anger in ways that will not hurt themselves or other people. When the anger and resentment are safely expressed, then we can begin to talk about forgiveness. It may take a long while before the anger is fully unloaded, but when it is, and the people are willing to forgive either themselves or another, then what takes place is a kind of radiance of new life and healing which could not otherwise happen. Those who come to us must decide when and if they are willing to dump their anger. They must decide when and if they are willing to move on to forgiveness. Given enough time, almost all the people with whom we have worked have come to this gracious willingness to forgive.

If you are interested in how forgiveness works in the lives of others, you may want to reread the stories written by Dana, Connie, Megan, Heather, and Linda.

Grief

Grief is an intense and acute emotional suffering that follows a traumatic loss. Most often our initial reaction to such a loss is shock, which may manifest itself as a deadening of all feelings, a moment of disbelief, or an emotional outburst and escalation of feelings. After the initial shock, a person will experience a number of feelings including sadness, anger, scare, and guilt.

Words frequently associated with grief include anguish, torment, distress, deep sorrow, mourning, and lamenting. Typical behavior includes shock, emotional paralysis, a sense of being frozen, weeping, rage, and a preoccupation with grief, guilt, or scare.

Unlike many feelings which go away quite quickly once they are faced and dealt with, grieving is a process which takes time to work through. Even when people have a good support system and do not allow their grief to deprive them of meaning, they often take about a year to grieve following a major loss.

The process of grieving is work, and it is never easy. Those who do it most effectively are those who are willing to handle themselves gently, to feel what they feel, to express those feelings and then let them go. Once they have accepted the reality of their loss, they are most likely to cry when they are sad, even if it seems as if they will never stop. They will stop when they have cried enough, although no one can tell just how long that will be.

These people will also accept their anger. They will find suitable ways to express their anger, such as talking about it, thrashing it out, yelling, screaming, writing about it, and becoming involved with energetic physical activities. When they feel scared they will get the reassurance they need, and if they feel guilty, they will do what they need to do to gain forgiveness. More detailed information on dealing with each of these feelings may be found in the sections on the respective feelings involved.

Another universal characteristic of grieving is a period of unpredictability. This is especially true at the beginning of the process. Those who are grieving are likely to wake up one morning feeling just fine and then by ten o'clock be furious or overcome with sadness or fear. Some people (especially those who think of themselves as predictable and level-headed) are likely to find these times of ups and downs the most difficult of all. However, this unexpected onslaught of distressing feelings that change from moment to moment is normal, and it is helpful to know that this will almost certainly happen.

Some people go on grieving for years and experience excessive problems. They become depressed, overwhelmed, hopeless, or helpless for long periods of time. There are three major reasons for prolonged or excessive grieving: 1) refusing to accept the reality of the loss; 2) accepting the loss but failing to allow the experience of the depth of the grief (denying the pain by putting on a brave front or deadening feelings with drugs or alcohol); 3) allowing the loss to cripple, and living permanently in an emotional wheelchair.

Those who do not accept the reality may go on for years acting as though the loss has not occurred. In her story Linda tells how miserable she was for so long after her doctor friend had left her. Although she was hurting and depressed, she had not accepted the fact that he was not available to her. When she first came to therapy the only thing she wanted was to find a magic wand to bring him back. But before her wounds could be healed she had to realize there was no magic. The relationship was dead. Once she accepted that, she could grieve and find new meaning for her own life.

In her story Connie tells how she refused to accept the fact that she had no hope of having a loving mother. As a result she kept on using her resources to find what was unattainable. Only when she was willing to accept the idea that she was never going to get what she wanted from her mother was she able to do her grieving. Then she started to discover how much love and acceptance was available to her from others.

Those who put on a brave front and refuse to allow themselves to feel the depth of their pain become prime candidates for ulcer, depression, workaholism, or alcoholism. Joy tells how she first struggled against accepting the fact that her marriage was over. Then, when she could deny it no longer, she did everything she could think of to try to get away from feeling her sense of abandonment, her anger, and her sadness. She went on an overseas trip, she moved to a new city, and kept herself busy working and going to classes, but years later she was still feeling guilty, still taking medication, still depressed, still suicidal. When she had the courage to look inside and face her rage she was able to deal with it and let it go, making room for forgiveness and self-acceptance once again.

Flora was a person who described herself as a "basket case." In our first interview she told how distressed she was because of the death of a child. She looked and acted as I would expect someone to in the early stages of grieving. Then she told me the child had died sixteen years before. I asked her to finish the sentence, "As long as I keep on suffering like this I do not need to...." She said, "stop being depressed." I then asked her to go on, "because if I stop being depressed, then I'll have to..." and she said, "accept that I wanted the child to die when I realized she was deformed." Flora now had to choose whether to go through the rest of her life continuing to be miserable or to do what needed to be done to resolve her guilt.

Note on
Religion and Psychotherapy

We are often asked how we think psychotherapy and religion are related. "Isn't it enough to have faith in God and then simply to pray for change and healing in one's life? Why go to a therapist?" Both authors of this book have had graduate training in theology as well as psychotherapy and this may be why we are asked this question, which is certainly an important one. To ask why a person of faith and prayer would want to have therapy is in some ways similar to asking why a person of faith and prayer would ever seek medical treatment. There are, of course, those who believe that medical treatment is unnecessary and that prayer is all one needs for physical healing. We have no quarrel with such people since we certainly know that faith and prayer may bring healing to both body and psyche.

If we look at this question in another way, however, we must ask a more basic question first. How does God work in our world? Both the Jewish and Christian religions teach that God is a God of history, that is, God is concerned with all of creation and has chosen to work in this world through men and women. Thus we become co-creators. God's work is accomplished through those whose faith enables them to be channels of divine power and love. In this view, then, the surgeon, the family doctor, the nurse, the lab technician all devote their medical skills for the patient's healing. Their skills, however, are God's gift to them for the healing of their patients' bodies. No one denies the hard work and dedication of those in medical healing, but some would say that all that any of us have or are is God's gracious gift to us.

In like manner, the therapist's training, skills, commitment, and work are God's gifts for healing broken psyches. A poet once wrote, "God has no hands but my hands to do His work today." We believe this is true of the work we do. In our book we have used very little "religious language." What we have written, however, is only about God's work: healing the sad, the lonely, the despairing, the broken in spirit.

A Final Word

We began this book by asking if anyone could really expect to have joy and wellness living as we do in our broken world. The authors' answer to this question is "yes." We would not continue in our profession as therapists if we did not believe that people can change and that they can move from desolation to joy, from worry to wellness.

In Part One you read stories written by people who had come to us for therapy because they had wanted to do just that—change their lives of anger, fear, and sadness for lives of hope, love, and joy. As you read their stories and the changes they made in their lives, you saw that facing their realities, taking charge of their lives, and choosing wellness was, for them, an exciting journey.

In Part Two we described how we worked as therapists with these people so that you might understand the kind of options that are open to you, if you should choose to work with a professional therapist.

In Part Three we invited you to take your own inner journey. To this end, we offered a number of practical suggestions and looked at ways you could develop an understanding of your own negative feelings so that you could change your life from one to worry to one of wellness.

Our time and effort in writing this book will be well rewarded if what we have written has been helpful to you.

The authors invite your comments on this book, both positive and negative. Write to Creative Living Associates, 204 N. Bayview Ave., Fairhope, AL 36532.